RAND McNALLY

Atlas
of American History
6th Edition

Editor
Brett R. Gover

Cartography
Rand McNally GIS Department

Writing
Elizabeth Leppman, PhD
Joella M. Morris

Product Management Director
Jenny Thornton

Design
Michelle LeBlanc-Smith

Production
Carey Seren

Photo credits
Cover images ©istockphoto
All interior images provided by ©2000 PhotoDisc, Inc.; p. 25 ©istockphoto / Getty, p. 63 ©Shutterstock.

Printed in U.S.A.
November 2025
PO# 79884

For information about ordering the Atlas of American History or the Atlas of American History Teacher's Guide, visit our website at **www.randmcnally.com/education**.

randpublishing.com

RAND McNALLY PUBLISHING

Introducing *Atlas of American History*

The features of *Atlas of American History* described below enhance understanding of America's past. They support and extend information from textbooks and primary sources. They provide additional links between history and geography.

Features of Atlas of American History

Historical Maps

Maps are arranged chronologically. Each map includes a title that describes its content and dates that indicate the period of history it shows. Compare maps of the same area in different time periods to view historical changes.

Map Legends and Labels

A map legend explains the colors and symbols used on a map. Historical maps often use solid or dashed lines to indicate routes of explorers or other groups of people. These routes may be labeled on the map. Labels also identify sites of historical events.

Captions

Each map has a caption that helps explain the content of the map. It may provide information about the historical context of the map or point out an important feature of the map. Legends, labels, and captions help tell the story of American history.

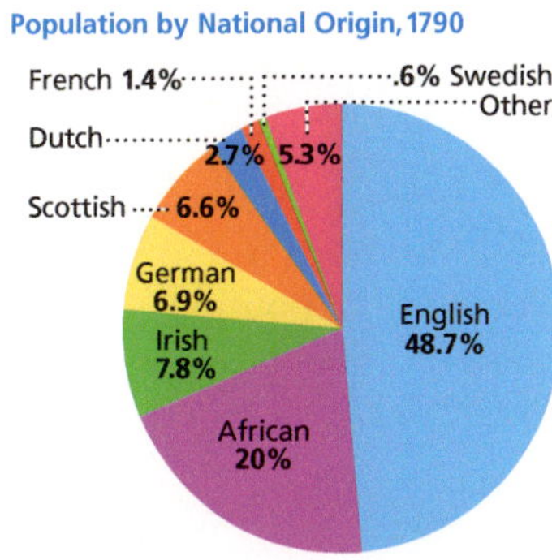

Some graphs in *Atlas of American History* illustrate information from the maps. Others provide additional information about American history. They may compare data or show changes over time.

Populations of United States Colonies and States, 1650-2020

States	1650	1700	1750	1770
Alabama				
Alaska				
Arizona				
Arkansas				
California				
Colorado				
Connecticut	4,139	25,970	111,280	183,881
Delaware	185	2,470	28,704	35,496

Databank

The databank is a reference section on pages 72-75 of the atlas. It provides tables of information about the United States and its people.

People — 1776 — Juan Bautista de Anza establishes a presidio at San Francisco.

Events — 1776 — Declaration of Independence is signed in Philadelphia.

Literature — 1776 — *"To His Excellency, General Washington,"* by a slave named Phillis Wheatley, is printed in the Pennsylvania Magazine.

Chronologies

Each section of *Atlas of American History* includes a chronology. It lists people, events, and literature associated with the time period represented on the maps in that section. These listings provide connections that aid understanding of history.

Index

The index is an alphabetical listing of the places and topics included in *Atlas of American History*. The index shows the page number(s) on which each entry appears. It provides explanatory information about many entries and refers to related entries when appropriate.

Periods of American History

Historians may divide American history into time periods in many different ways. Some periods may center around a theme, such as exploration. Others may center around an important event, such as the American Revolution.

Rand McNally *Atlas of American History* is divided into sections based on time periods described below. Some periods overlap to provide coverage of political and social history. Maps are organized chronologically within each section.

1. Beginnings (prehistory-1620)

Thousands of years ago, hunters from Asia migrated to the lands now called the Americas. These people, now referred to as American Indians or Native Americans, settled throughout the continents. They developed many different cultures, depending upon the environments in which they lived. They remained the only people in the Western Hemisphere until about A.D. 1000, when Vikings from Norway migrated to the coast of North America.

During the 1400s, European demand for Asian goods led Columbus to sail west across the Atlantic Ocean in search of a route to Asia. His discovery of a world previously unknown to Europeans touched off an age of exploration. During the 1500s, Europeans explored and claimed land in the Americas.

2. Establishing Colonies (1600-1775)

During the 1600s and early 1700s, Europeans came to the Americas for many different reasons. English settlers came seeking the freedom to worship as they pleased. Spaniards came to find gold and to spread Christianity. French trappers came to establish fur trade. Dutch settlers came for the promise of land. In addition, many Africans were brought to the Americas as slaves.

By the mid-1700s, English claims extended along the Atlantic coast, and the French controlled the vast interior of North America. Britain and France competed for control of the continent. As a result of the French and Indian War (1754-1763), Britain gained Canada and all of North America east of the Mississippi River.

3. Forming a New Nation (1775-1800)

English settlers in North America developed a prosperous economy and a way of life that differed from that in Great Britain. They began to resent Britain's control. They declared their independence and fought a revolution to win their freedom. As a result, the United States became an independent nation.

The original thirteen states stretched along the Atlantic coast. The western boundary of the new nation extended to the Mississippi River. Americans began to settle lands west of the Appalachian Mountains. The national government passed laws providing for the sale of western lands and the addition of new states.

4. The Nation Expands & Changes (1790-1870)

Much of the history of the United States is a story of westward movement. Between 1803 and 1848, the nation expanded its boundaries from the Mississippi River to the Pacific Coast. Pioneers had settled most of the land east of the Mississippi River by 1840.

	1769	**1804**	**1933**
People	Junípero Serra starts first Spanish mission in what is now California.	Meriwether Lewis and William Clark lead expedition from St. Louis to the Pacific Ocean.	President Franklin Roosevelt creates TVA to develop the natural resources of the Tennessee Valley.
	about 700 B.C.	**1565**	**1787**
Events	The Adena (early North American Indians) build mounds in what is now Ohio.	Spaniards establish St. Augustine, FL, first permanent European settlement in what is now the United States.	Founders write the U.S. Constitution in Philadelphia, PA.
	1608	**1704**	**1868**
Literature	*A True Relation of Occurrences in Virginia*, by John Smith, describes the founding of Jamestown.	Sarah Kemble Knight's *Journal* describes the author's horseback journey from Boston to New York.	*Little Women*, by Louisa May Alcott, tells the story of four sisters growing up in New England in the mid-1800s.

In the early 1800s, fur trappers, traders, and miners pushed west of the Mississippi River, seeking economic opportunities. Soon they were followed by farmers and ranchers who settled the land. The promise of land and the hope of a better life also attracted millions of European immigrants to the United States.

5. A Nation Divided (1850-1865)

Different ways of life developed in the North and the South. Southern agriculture was based on slave labor. Industrial states in the North outlawed slavery. As settlers moved westward, new states were created. The question of whether to allow slavery in the new states led to conflict between the North and the South.

Debate and compromise failed to solve the problems. Eleven southern states withdrew from the Union. Between 1861 and 1865, the North and the South fought against each other in the Civil War.

6. Emerging as a Modern Nation (1860-1920)

Within 25 years after the Civil War ended, the process of settling the United States from coast to coast was completed. The settlement of the West also brought an end to the Native American way of life. The federal government sent soldiers to stop uprisings and move Indians onto reservations.

As the United States became an industrial nation, people moved to cities to work in factories. Millions of European immigrants also came to the United States seeking jobs.

The nation acquired territories overseas and began to emerge as a modern nation. By fighting in World War I, the United States also proved that it had become a world power.

7. Challenges & Changes in the 20th Century (1920-1999)

A period of prosperity followed World War I. However, the stock market crash in 1929 plunged the nation into an economic depression that lasted throughout the 1930s. During those years, the actions of powerful dictators in Europe led to World War II.

The United States fought in World War II from 1941 to 1945. It emerged as the leader of the free world, and the Soviet Union emerged as the leader of the Communist world. During the following decades, the United States intervened in many parts of the world to stop the spread of Communism. The Cold War finally ended in 1991.

8. Entering a New Millennium (2000 and beyond)

The United States has compiled information about the American population every ten years since 1790, when the first census was taken. According to the 2020 census, more than three-fourths of the country's 330 million people lived in cities. Americans born in 2000 could expect to live longer than any previous generation. Although many Americans lived in poverty in 2020, the United States had one of the world's highest standards of living.

The United States faces many challenges as it enters a new millennium. It must meet the needs of its diverse population. It must also continue its role of leadership in a rapidly changing world. The story of America is ongoing because today's events will become tomorrow's history.

1955
Rosa Parks protests segregation in Montgomery, AL by refusing to give up bus seat to white passenger.

1969
U.S. astronaut Neil Armstrong becomes first person to walk on the moon.

2001
Colin Powell, son of Jamaican immigrants, becomes first African American to serve as U.S. Secretary of State.

1848
Discovery of gold in California brings settlers to the West.

1941
Japanese bombing of Pearl Harbor, Hawaii, brings U.S. into World War II.

1970
Americans participate in Earth Day, a nationwide demonstration of concern for the environment.

1932
Little House in the Big Woods, by Laura Ingalls Wilder, describes life in the Midwest in the 1870s and 1880s.

1976
Roots: The Saga of an American Family, by Alex Haley, traces the author's ancestry back to the African slave trade.

2012
Home, by Toni Morrison, becomes the author's tenth novel chronicling African American community life.

Benefits of Using Rand McNally *Atlas of American History*

Events gain fuller meaning.

Knowing where events took place gives them fuller meaning and often explains causes and effects. For example, the map of the final campaign of the American Revolution, on page 27, shows how American and French forces trapped the British at Yorktown. It helps explain why Cornwallis surrendered.

Connections among events are clarified.

Through the visual power of historical maps, the links between and among events become clear. The maps on pages 12 and 13 show international trade routes, 1350-1450, and Portuguese routes to India in the 1400s. They help explain why Europeans wanted to find an all-water route to Asia. They provide the background to understanding the age of exploration that followed Columbus's discovery of the Americas.

Similarities and differences become apparent.

The maps in *Atlas of American History* provide an opportunity to compare and contrast places over time. Compare the map of North America in 1763, on page 23, with the map of North America in 1783 on page 28. These maps show the emergence of the United States on a continent claimed by Britain and Spain.

The maps in this atlas also provide an opportunity to compare and contrast regions of the United States. The map titled "A Quarreling People," on page 41, indicates differences between the North and the South at the time of the Civil War.

The influence of sense of place is conveyed.

Maps in *Atlas of American History* convey people's sense of place at a particular time in history. The map titled "Opportunities and Uncertainties," on page 58, is a good example. The map's polar projection emphasizes how near the Soviet Union is to the United States. It reflects Americans' fear of nuclear attack from the north during the postwar period of tension between the United States and the Soviet Union.

Trends emerge.

The maps in this atlas show trends in American history. The map of Westward Expansion, on pages 36-37, shows the sequence in which the United States acquired land. It indicates the westward movement of settlement patterns. The maps on pages 38, 48, and 61 indicate changing trends in immigration.

The story of American history is communicated.

The text in *Atlas of American History* presents a chronological overview of American history and summarizes key events. It provides cross curricular connections by listing literature that clarifies or expands historical understandings. It highlights people whose accomplishments reflect American ideals.

The *Did You Know?* feature on each section opening page provides an interesting sidelight to history. Like the example below, each of these features demonstrates how history has influenced the American experience.

Did You Know

A picture of the Greek god Atlas supporting the earth on his shoulders appeared on the title page of an early book of maps. Later, people began to call a collection of maps an atlas.

Section 1 | (Prehistory-1620)

The Cliff Palace in Mesa Verde, Colorado, was built by the Anasazi around 1100.

In 1524, Verrazano explored the Atlantic coast of what is now North Carolina.

To learn about **prehistory**, or the time before human beings learned to write, scientists study the physical evidence that early people left behind. This evidence suggests the first Americans migrated from Asia between 25,000 and 8,000 years ago. The descendants of these people, now called Native Americans spread throughout the Americas and developed different cultures.

Historical evidence indicates that Vikings from Norway established a settlement in North America about A.D. 1000. During the 1400s, increased demand for Asian goods led European nations to seek a water route to Asia. Columbus was attempting to achieve this goal when he discovered a world previously unknown to Europeans.

During the 1500s, European explorers who came to the Americas found continents inhabited by native peoples of diverse cultures, from hunters and gatherers to advanced civilizations. Although figures vary greatly, the graph at the right indicates estimates of Native American populations around that time.

Estimates of Native American Populations in 1492

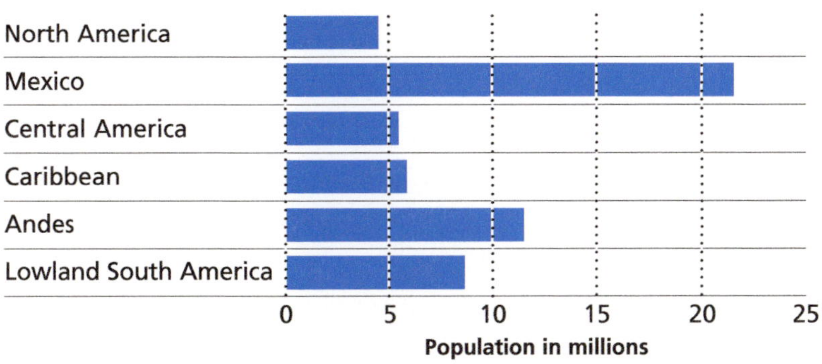

Did You Know

Scientists discovered a spearhead among bones of ancient bison near Folsom, New Mexico. These animals became extinct about 10,000 years ago. This discovery proved people had migrated to the region by about 8000 B.C.

	about A.D. 1000	**1492**	**1587**
People	Leif Ericson establishes a Viking settlement on the east coast of North America.	Christopher Columbus lands on San Salvador.	Virginia Dare, first English child born in America, is born on Roanoke Island.
	about 23,000 B.C.	**1325**	**about 1570**
Events	First Americans probably migrate from Asia to North America.	Aztecs build Tenochtitlán on site of present-day Mexico City.	Five Indian tribes in what is now New York form League of the Iroquois.
	1298	**1504**	**1552**
Literature	*Description of the World*, by Marco Polo, tells of the Italian trader's journey from Venice to China.	*New World*, a letter by Amerigo Vespucci, becomes the basis for naming America.	*In Defense of the Indian*, by Bartolomé de Las Casas, criticizes the Spanish for abusing Indians on Hispaniola.

During the Ice Ages, much of Earth's water was frozen in glaciers. These huge ice sheets covered much of what is now Canada and the northern United States. Scientists believe a land bridge existed where the Bering Strait now separates Asia and Alaska. Between 25,000 and 10,000 years ago, people from Asia may have migrated across the land bridge and spread throughout North America and South America.

a

About A.D. 1000, Norwegian Vikings, who had settled in Greenland, explored the coast of North America. They established a settlement in what is now Newfoundland, Canada.

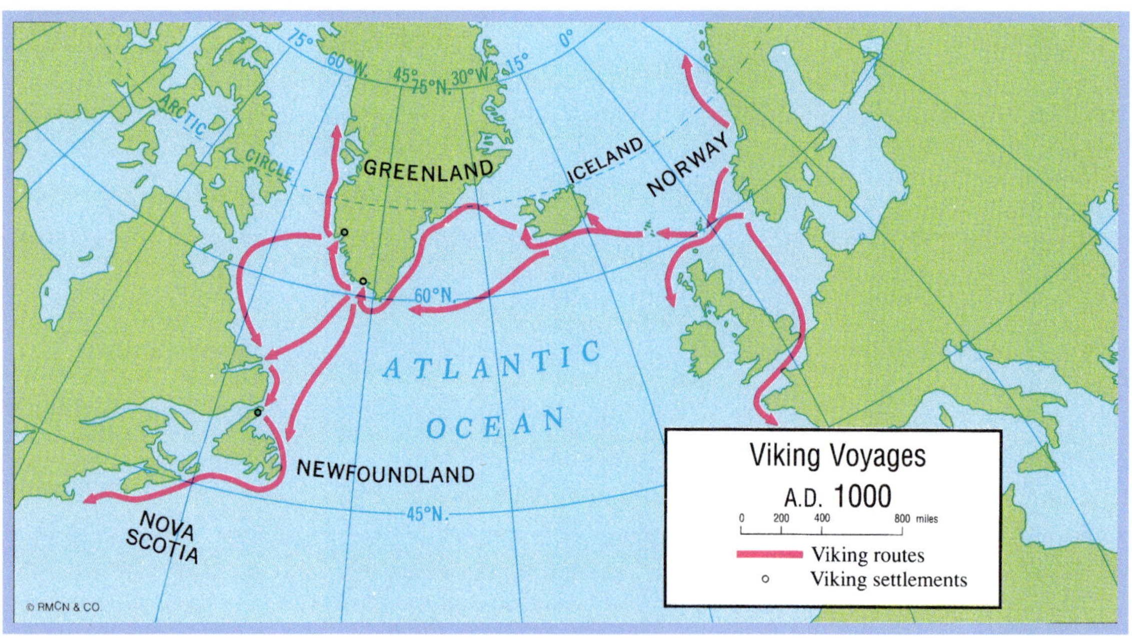

b

▲ Environments in which tribes of Native Americans followed a similar way of life are called culture areas. The culture areas shown on the map existed around 1500, when Europeans began to arrive in the Americas. The map also lists major tribes of Native Americans within each culture area.

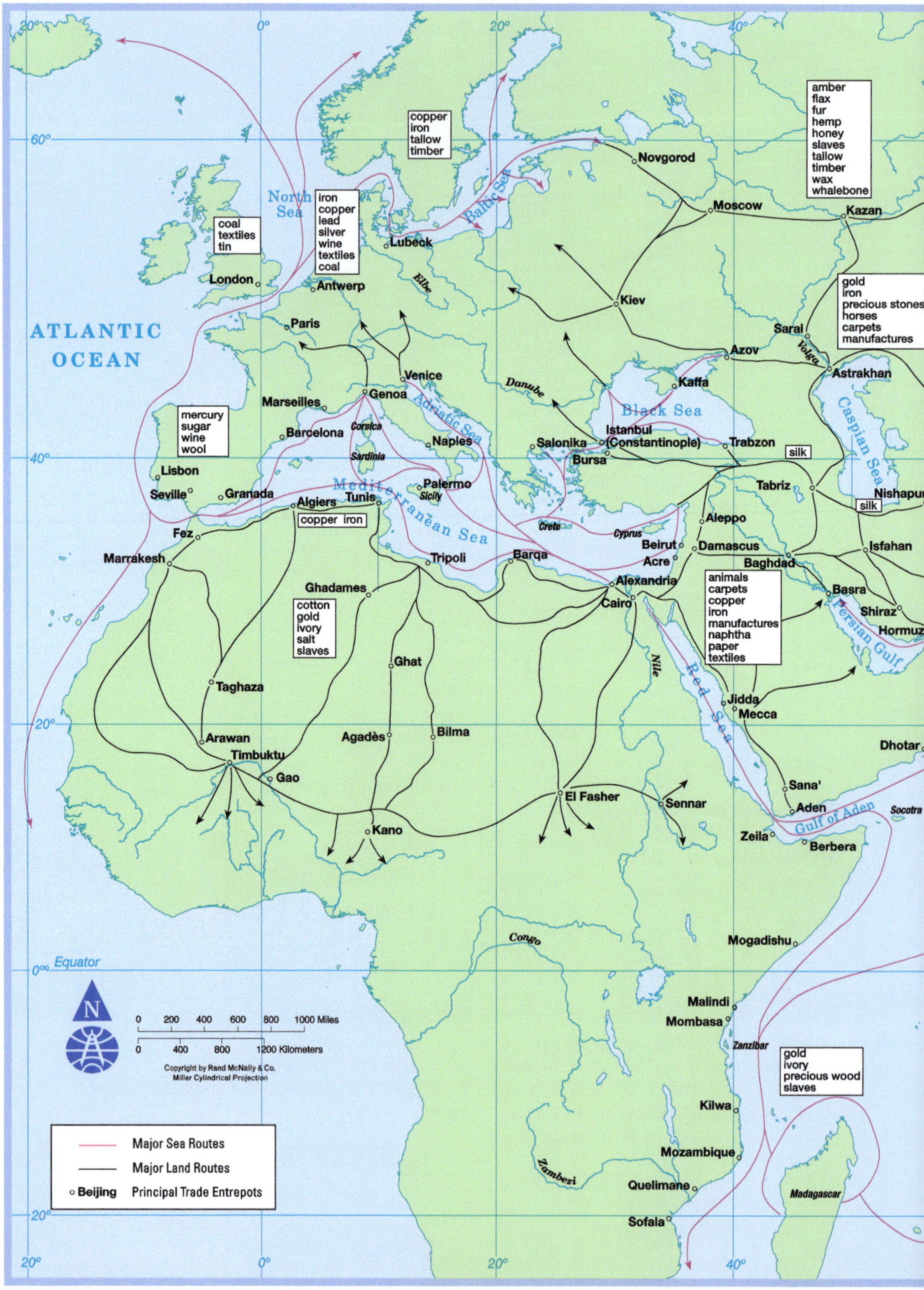
ATLANTIC OCEAN
North Sea
Baltic Sea
Black Sea
Caspian Sea
Adriatic Sea
Mediterranean Sea
Red Sea
Persian Gulf
Gulf of Aden
Elbe
Danube
Volga
Nile
Congo
Zambezi
Corsica
Sardinia
Sicily
Crete
Cyprus
Socotra
Zanzibar
Madagascar
Equator
copper
iron
tallow
timber
amber
flax
fur
hemp
honey
slaves
tallow
timber
wax
whalebone
coal
textiles
tin
iron
copper
lead
silver
wine
textiles
coal
gold
iron
precious stones
horses
carpets
manufactures
mercury
sugar
wine
wool
copper iron
silk
silk
cotton
gold
ivory
salt
slaves
animals
carpets
copper
iron
manufactures
naphtha
paper
textiles
gold
ivory
precious wood
slaves
Novgorod
Moscow
Kazan
Lubeck
London
Antwerp
Paris
Kiev
Saral
Astrakhan
Azov
Kaffa
Venice
Genoa
Marseilles
Barcelona
Naples
Salonika
Istanbul (Constantinople)
Bursa
Trabzon
Lisbon
Seville
Granada
Algiers
Tunis
Palermo
Tabriz
Nishapur
Aleppo
Isfahan
Fez
Marrakesh
Tripoli
Barqa
Beirut
Acre
Damascus
Baghdad
Basra
Shiraz
Hormuz
Alexandria
Cairo
Ghadames
Ghat
Taghaza
Jidda
Mecca
Arawan
Timbuktu
Agadès
Bilma
Dhotar
Gao
El Fasher
Sennar
Sana'
Aden
Kano
Zeila
Berbera
Mogadishu
Malindi
Mombasa
Kilwa
Mozambique
Quelimane
Sofala
0 200 400 600 800 1000 Miles
0 400 800 1200 Kilometers
Copyright by Rand McNally & Co.
Miller Cylindrical Projection
Major Sea Routes
Major Land Routes
Beijing Principal Trade Entrepots

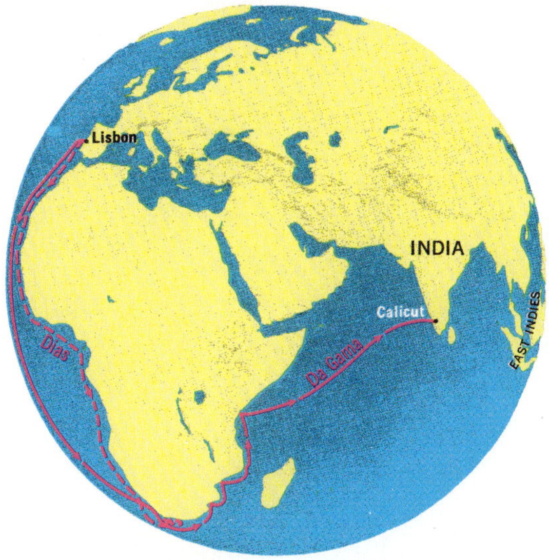

Portuguese Routes to India 1488-1498

Between 1350 and 1450, Italian cities controlled trade through the Mediterranean, and Turkish Muslims controlled the main overland routes between Europe and Asia. Demand for Asian goods led European nations to seek a water route to Asia. The globe shows the routes of Portuguese explorers who accomplished this goal. In 1488 Bartholomeu Dias sailed around the southern tip of Africa. Ten years later, Vasco de Gama sailed around Africa to India.

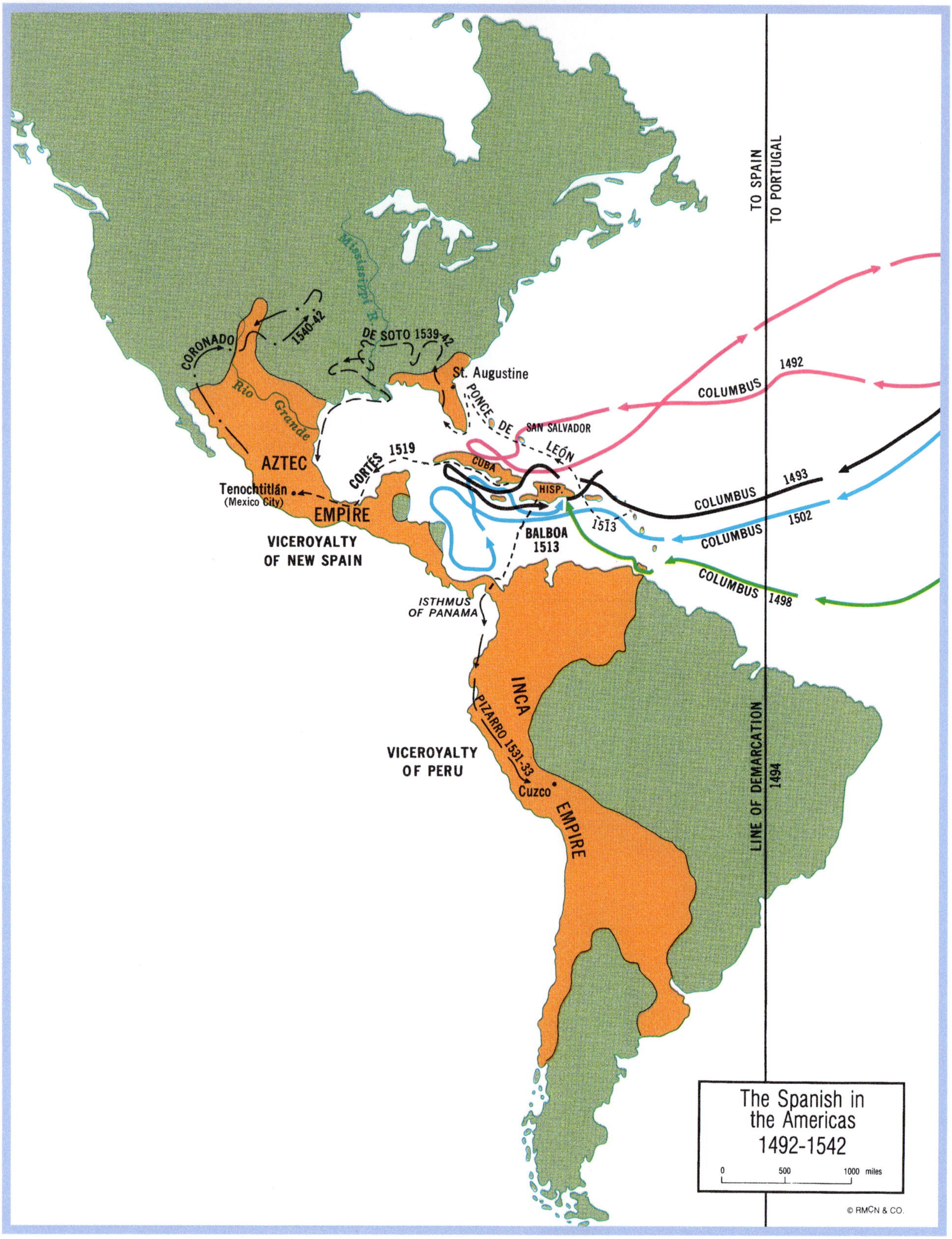

The voyages of Christopher Columbus led other Europeans to explore the Americas. Pope Alexander VI established the Line of Demarcation to prevent disputes between Spain and Portugal over lands their explorers claimed. The Spanish conquered Indian empires in Mexico and Peru.

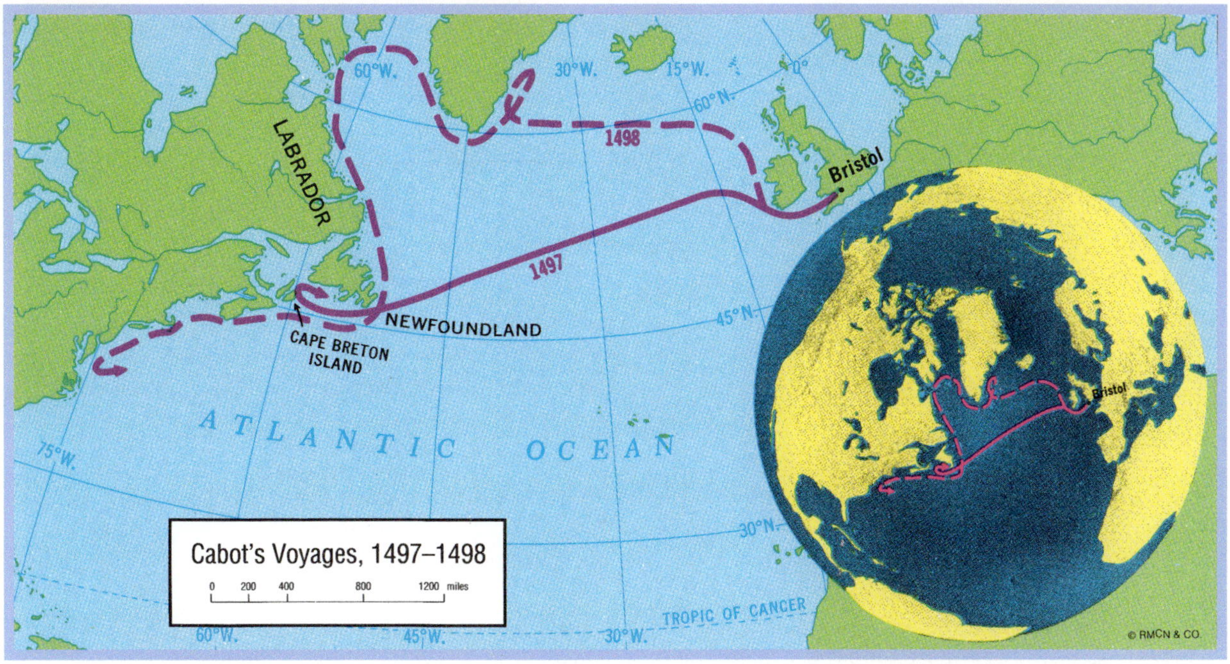

a

John Cabot attempted to reach Asia by a northwest route across the Atlantic Ocean. In 1497 and 1498, Cabot explored the coasts of present-day Labrador, Newfoundland, and Cape Breton Island (Nova Scotia). His voyages gave England a claim to North America.

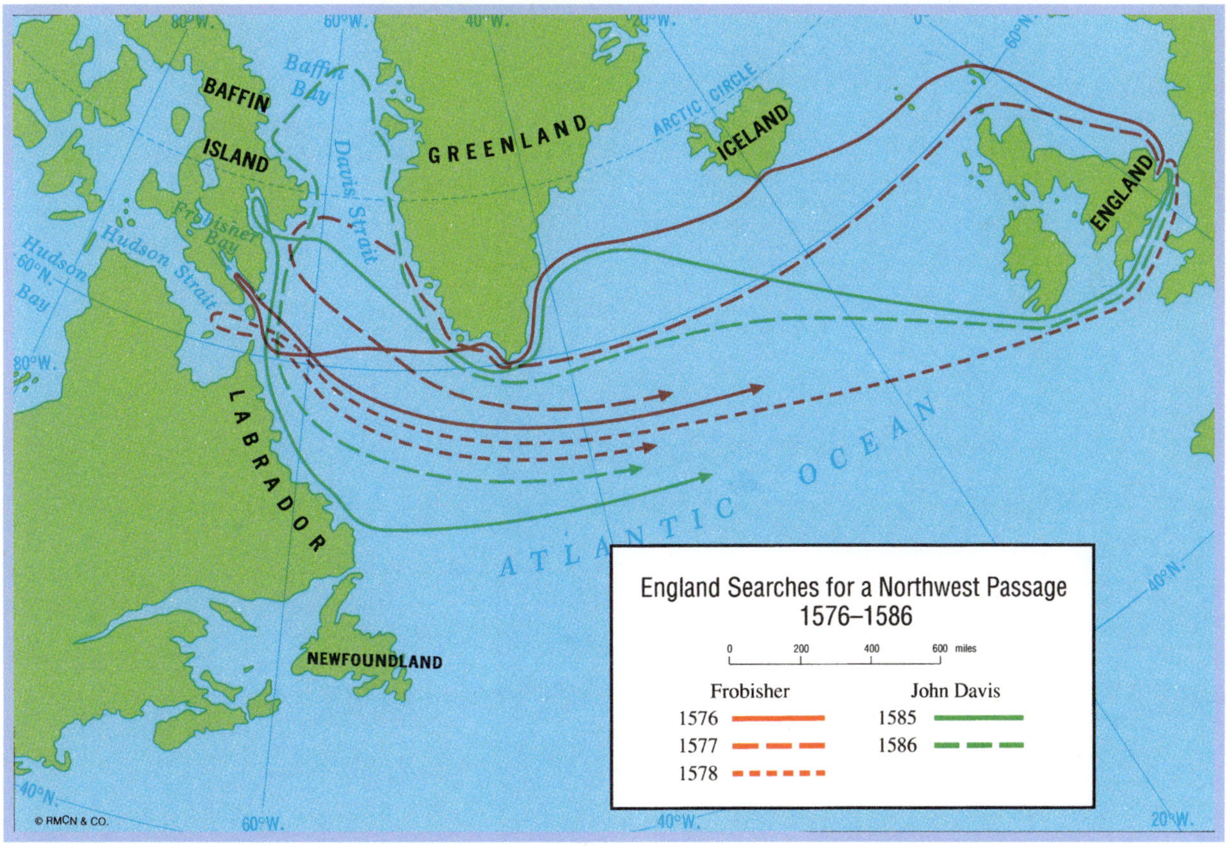

b

In the 1570s and 1580s, England renewed its search for a water route to Asia through North America. Martin Frobisher and John Davis explored the Atlantic coast of what is now Canada and the area between Greenland and Baffin Island.

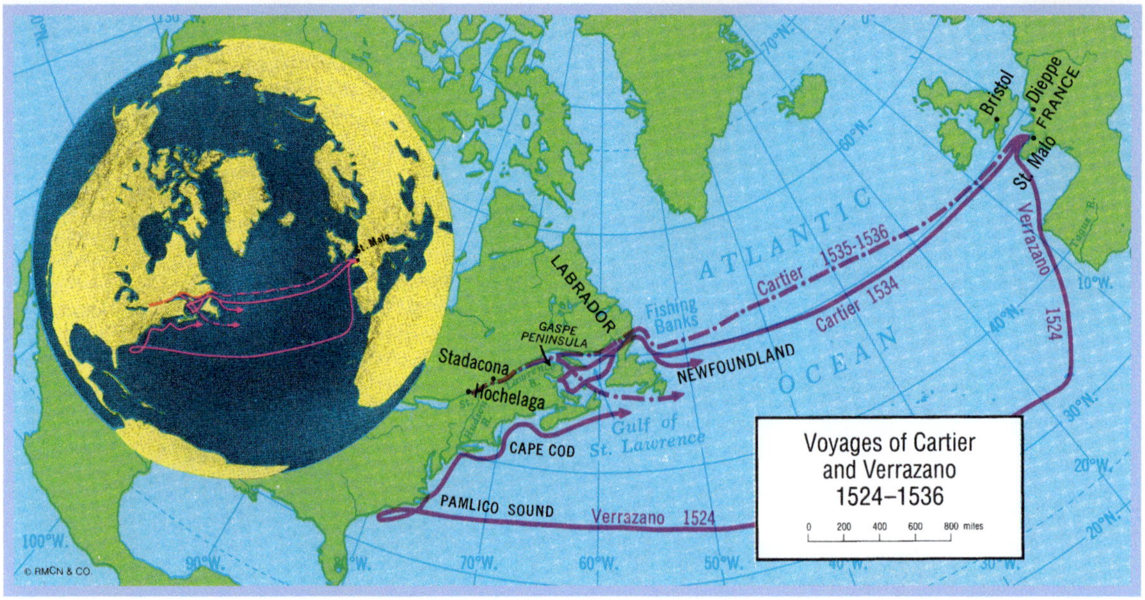

a

France also sent explorers in search of a water route through North America. Giovanni da Verrazano explored the Atlantic coast from what is now North Carolina to Newfoundland. Jacques Cartier explored the St. Lawrence River and claimed the region for France.

b

Samuel de Champlain extended French claims in North America. In 1608 he founded the city of Quebec. He then helped the Algonquin and Huron Indians defeat the Iroquois. Etienne Brulé lived among the Huron Indians and explored the river systems of northeastern North America for France.

Section 2 | (1600-1775)

This stone canopy stands near the Massachusetts shore. It covers Plymouth Rock, which marks the spot near which the Pilgrims are believed to have stepped ashore.

Reproductions of ships that brought the first settlers to Jamestown are on the James River in Virginia. They are near the site of the first permanent British settlement in America.

Between 1600 and 1775, Europeans established **colonies**, or settlements ruled by their homelands, in North America. The British settled along the Atlantic coast and eventually took over Dutch and Swedish colonies established there. By 1732, thirteen British colonies stretched along the east coast of the present United States from New Hampshire to Georgia.

The French claimed the vast interior of North America. British attempts to settle west of the Appalachians led to conflict between France and Great Britain. The French and Indian War gave Great Britain control of all land east of the Mississippi River.

The colonial population grew rapidly due to a high birth rate and increased immigration. People came to America seeking religious freedom and economic opportunities. Slave traders also brought thousands of unwilling immigrants from Africa.

Did You Know

Swedish settlers introduced log cabins in America. They built these houses along the Delaware River in the 1640s.

Growth of Colonial Population

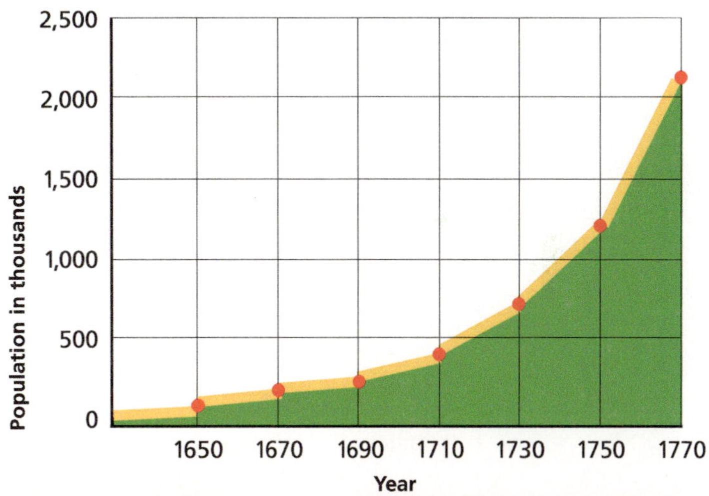

	1614	1626	1682
People	Pocahontas, daughter of Chief Powhatan, marries Jamestown colonist John Rolfe.	Peter Minuit purchases Manhattan Island from Indigenous people.	LaSalle claims Mississippi River Valley for France.
	1607	**1620**	**1754**
Events	Jamestown is founded.	Pilgrims settle Plymouth Colony.	French and Indian War begins at Fort Necessity.
	1640	**1650**	**1733**
Literature	The *Bay Psalm Book* is the first book written and published in the American colonies.	*The Tenth Muse Lately Sprung Up in America*, by Anne Bradstreet, describes home life in colonial New England.	*Poor Richard's Almanack*, by Ben Franklin, is published in Philadelphia.

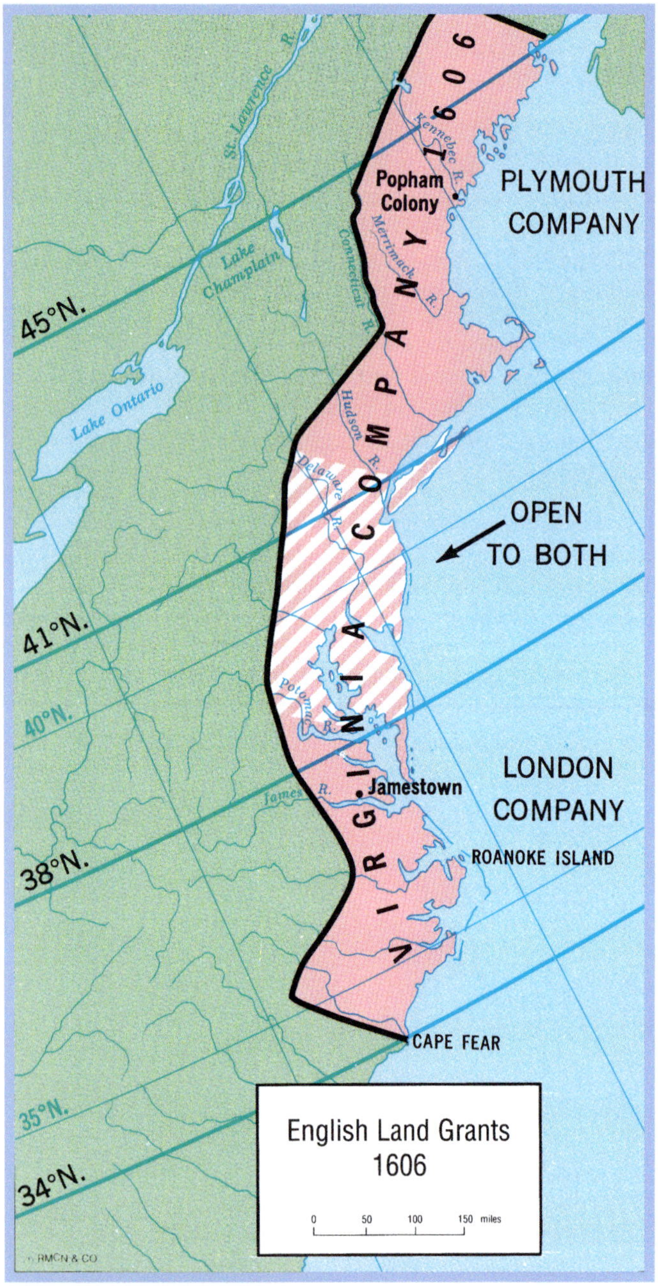

▲ The Plymouth Company and the London Company were groups of stockholders within the Virginia Company. Each group obtained a land grant from the English king to establish a colony in America. Land between 38° and 41° north latitude was open to both groups. Neither group was allowed to settle within 100 miles of the other. **a**

▲ The Dutch bought Manhattan Island from Native Americans and established a fortified trading center called New Amsterdam. They established other settlements along the Hudson River and later took over Swedish settlements along the Delaware River. **b**

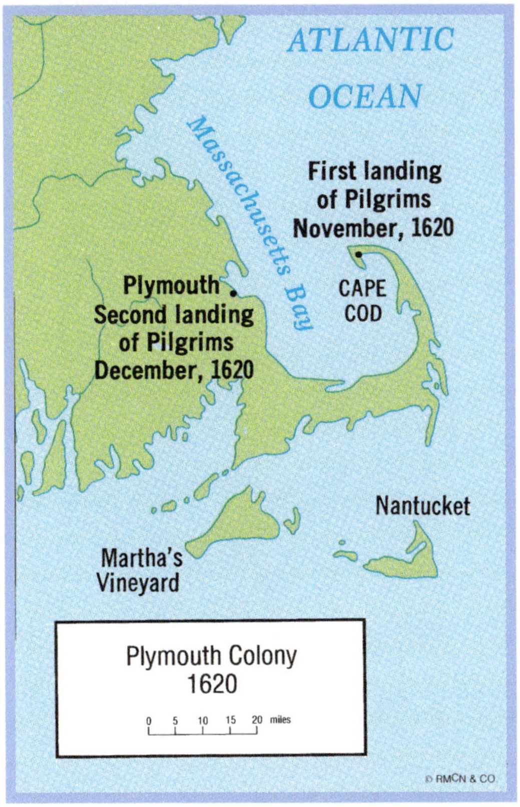

a

▲ The Pilgrims named their colony Plymouth, after the English port from which they had sailed.

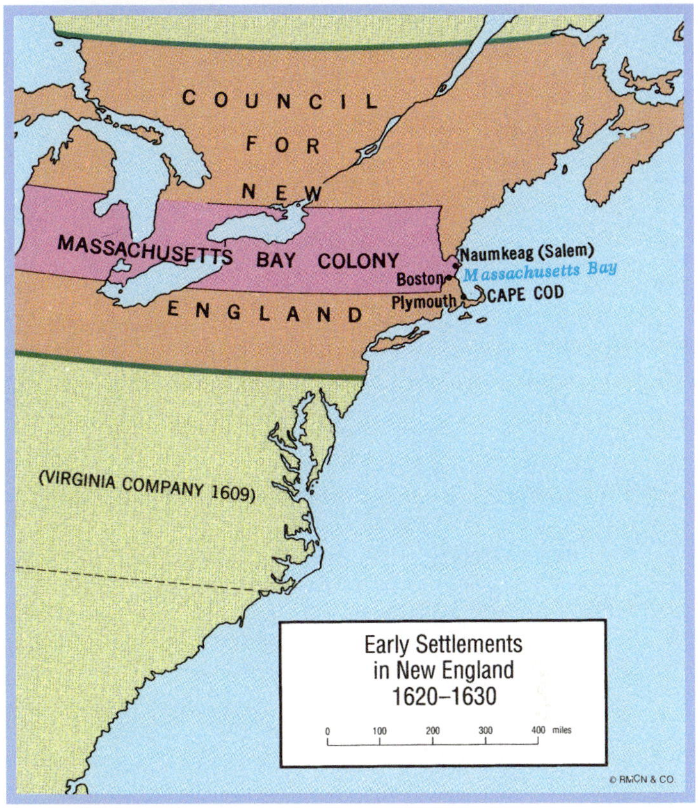

b

▲ In 1620 a group called the Council for New England received a land grant from the English king. The Massachusetts Bay Colony was established on this land in 1628.

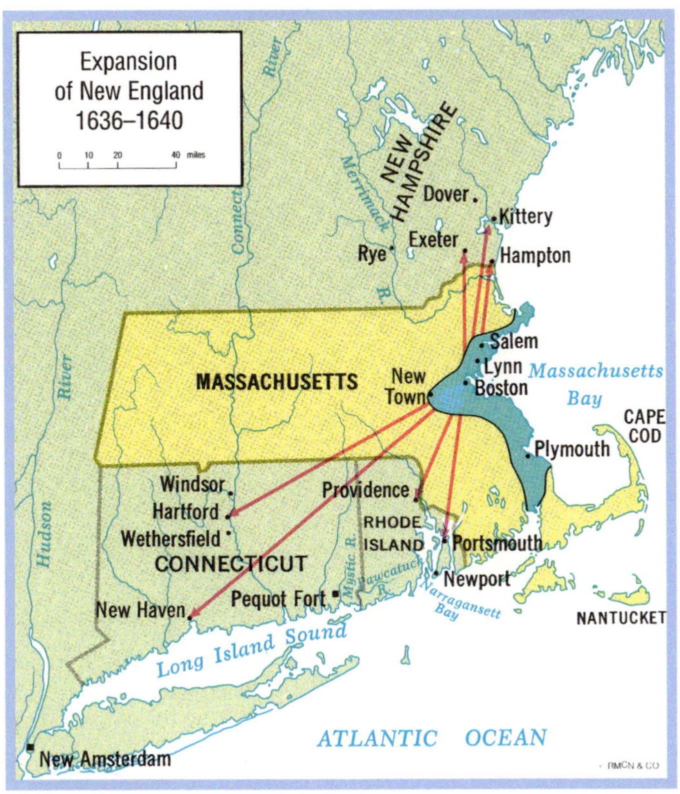

c

◀ The Puritans established settlements in the eastern part of Massachusetts, shown in blue on the map. Plymouth became part of the Massachusetts Colony. People who disagreed with Puritan views left Massachusetts and established new colonies.

France claimed the vast interior of North America, but it had little control over the region because of a lack of settlers.

▲ In about 150 years, the British established the 13 colonies that would become the United States. By 1750 the British colonies had a population of more than 1 million.

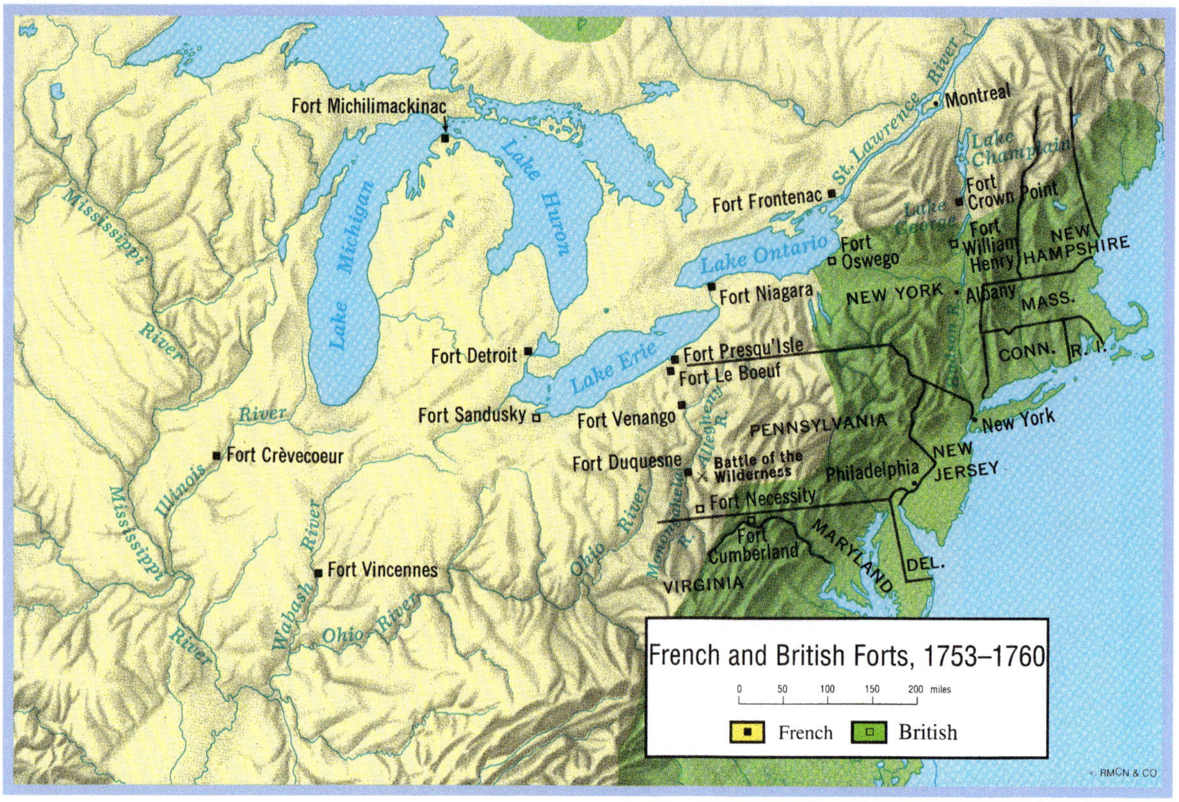

a

▲ To keep the British east of the Appalachians, the French built a string of forts from Lake Erie to the Ohio River.

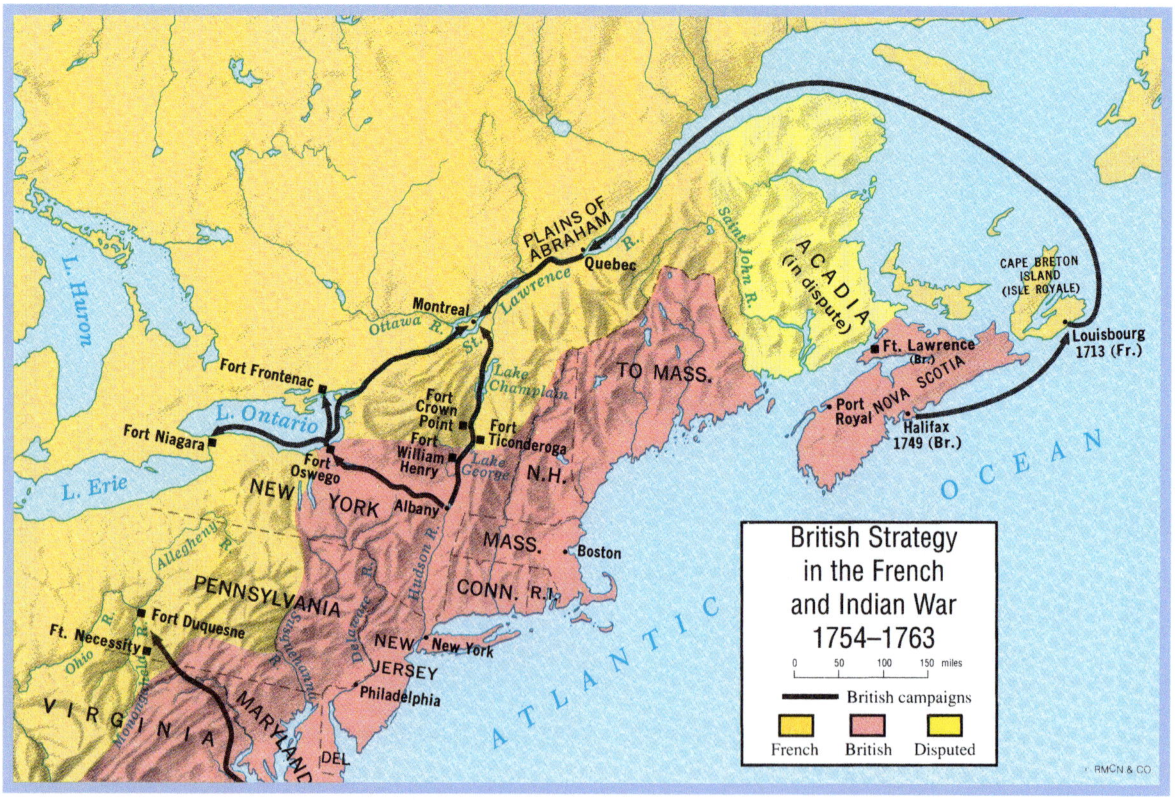

b

▲ The British captured French forts in the St. Lawrence Valley and the eastern Great Lakes region.

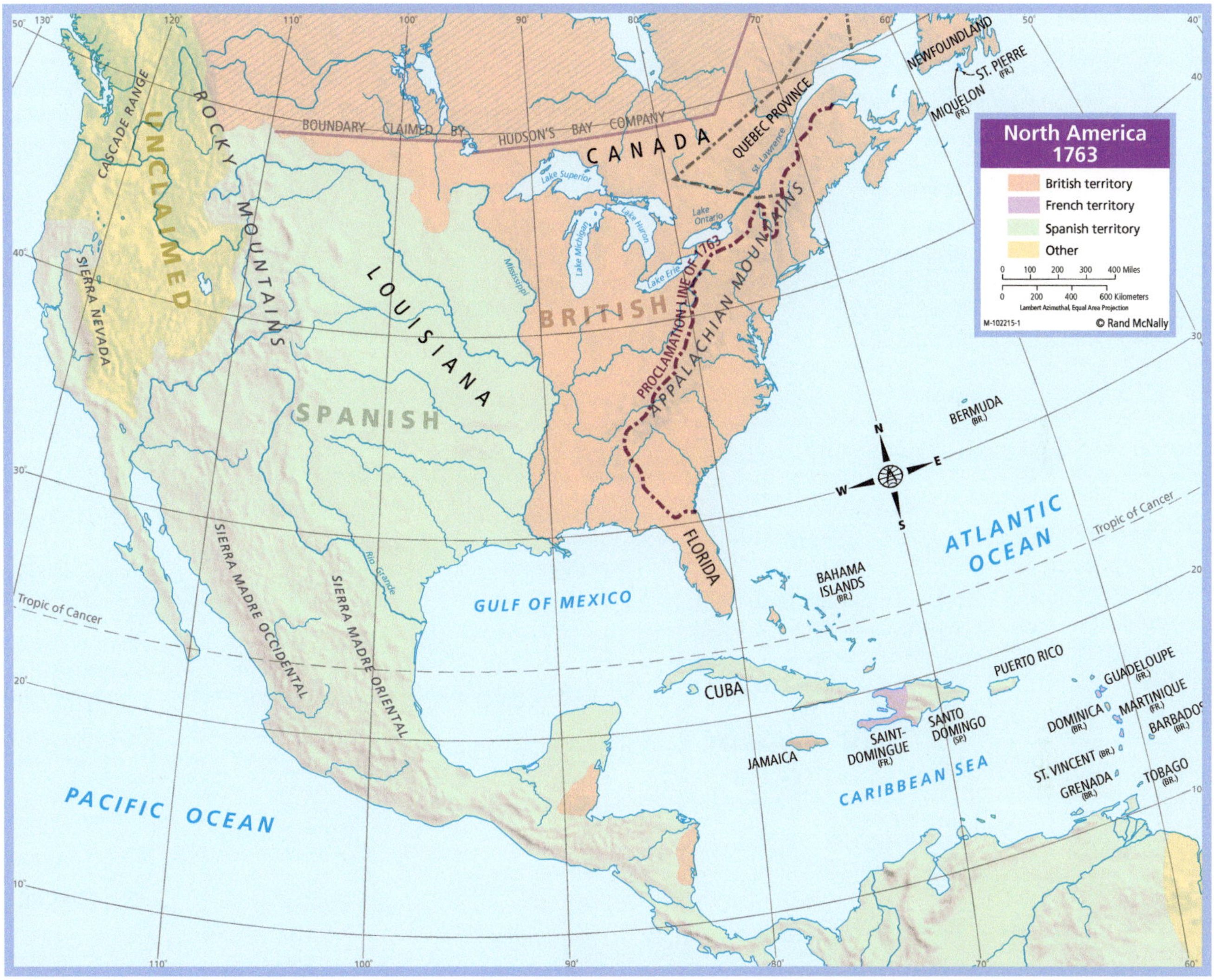

▲ The French and Indian War ended French control in North America. According to the Treaty of Paris in 1763, France kept only a few islands in the Caribbean. Great Britain acquired Canada and all French lands east of the Mississippi River. From Spain, France's ally in the war, Great Britain acquired Florida. To make up for the loss of Florida, France gave Spain the vast land between the Mississippi River and the Rocky Mountains.

Some colonial trade involved the exchange of goods for slaves. Thousands of unwilling immigrants from Africa suffered terribly during the voyage to America.

Section 3 | (1775-1800)

This statue in Boston honors Paul Revere's historic ride on April 18, 1775. Revere rode from Boston to Lexington to warn colonists that the British were coming.

During the 1700s, Spanish explorers built missions, like the one shown here, throughout the southwestern part of the present United States.

Between 1775 and 1800, the United States became an independent nation and established a new government. The Revolutionary War began when American minutemen clashed with British soldiers at Lexington and Concord in 1775. It ended in 1781 when General George Washington's troops, aided by French forces, defeated General Charles Cornwallis and his British troops at Yorktown.

The Treaty of Paris of 1783 recognized the independence of the United States and established its borders. The nation extended from the Atlantic Coast to the Mississippi River. The new states **ceded**, or gave up, their western lands to the federal government. The government created the Northwest Territory and provided for the sale of land to settlers.

The Constitution, ratified in 1788, established the government that remains in effect today. The census in 1790 indicated the national origins of the American population.

Population by National Origin, 1790

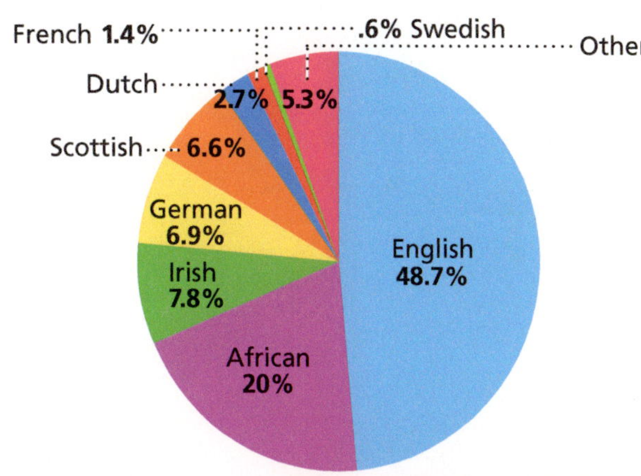

Did You Know

The states carved from the Northwest Territory might be different if Thomas Jefferson had named them. He suggested such names as Dolypotamia, Assinisippia, and Metropotamia.

People	**1776** Juan Bautista de Anza establishes a presidio at San Francisco.	**1789** George Washington takes presidential oath of office in New York.	**1791** Benjamin Banneker, an African American surveyor, helps plan Washington, D.C.
Events	**1776** Declaration of Independence is signed in Philadelphia.	**1785** Land Ordinance provides plan for sale of land in the Northwest Territory.	**1800** Washington, D.C. becomes the national capital.
Literature	**1776** "To His Excellency George Washington," by a slave named Phillis Wheatley, is printed in the Philadelphia Magazine.	**1782** *Letters from an American Farmer*, by Jean de Crèvecoeur, describes social customs in the United States.	**1787** *The Federalist*, by Hamilton, Madison, and Jay, urges New York to ratify the Constitution.

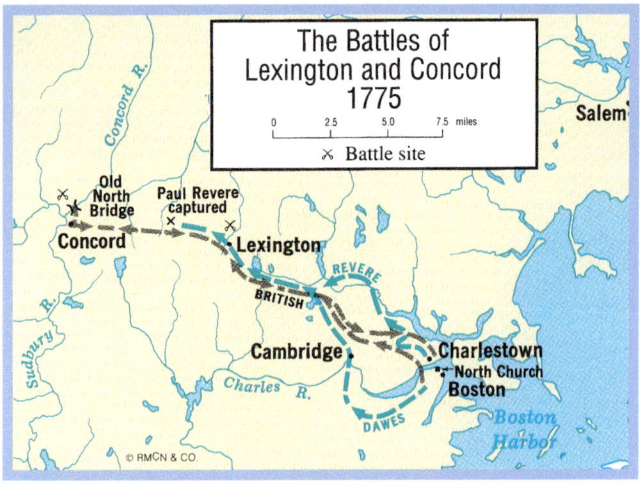

On the way to Concord, the British were met at Lexington by minutemen who had been warned by William Dawes and Paul Revere. a

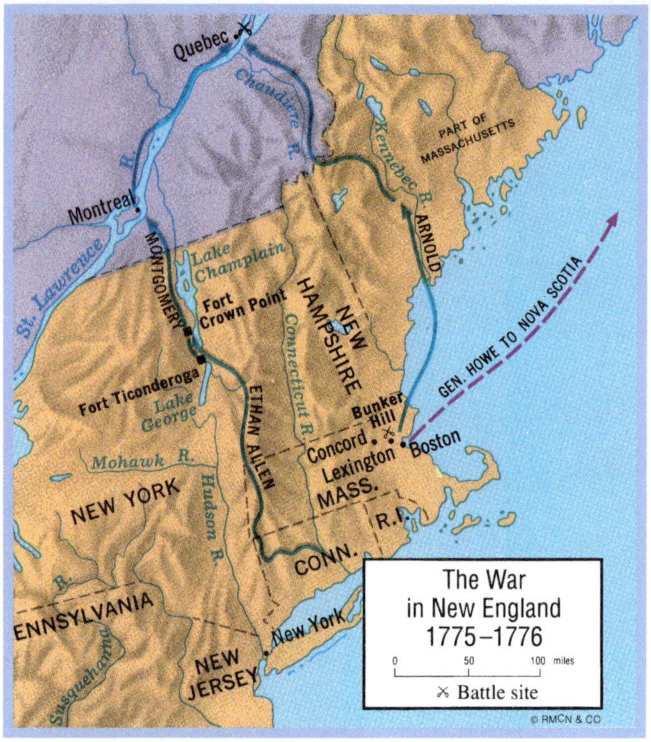

Americans captured British artillery at Forts Ticonderoga and Crown Point. They used the cannons in Boston, where they forced General William Howe and his troops to leave. An American invasion of Canada, led by Generals Richard Montgomery and Benedict Arnold, failed. b

The British victory on Long Island forced George Washington and his troops to retreat from New York. After victories at Trenton and Princeton, American troops moved to winter quarters at Morristown. c

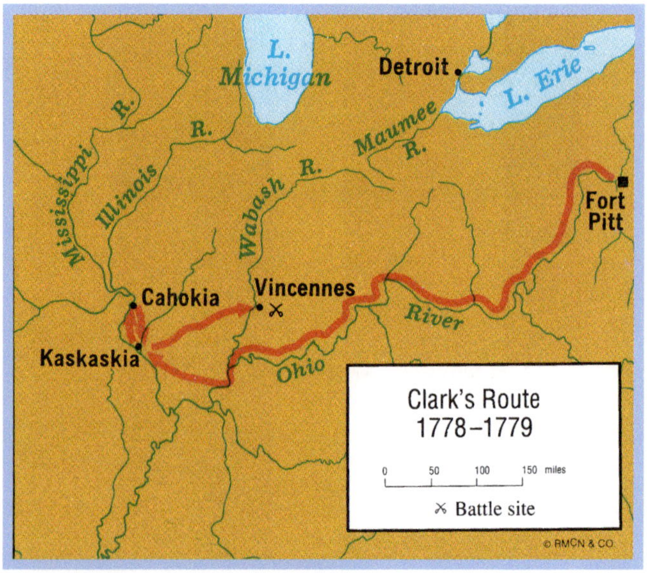

Troops led by George Rogers Clark captured British settlements in the Ohio Valley. d

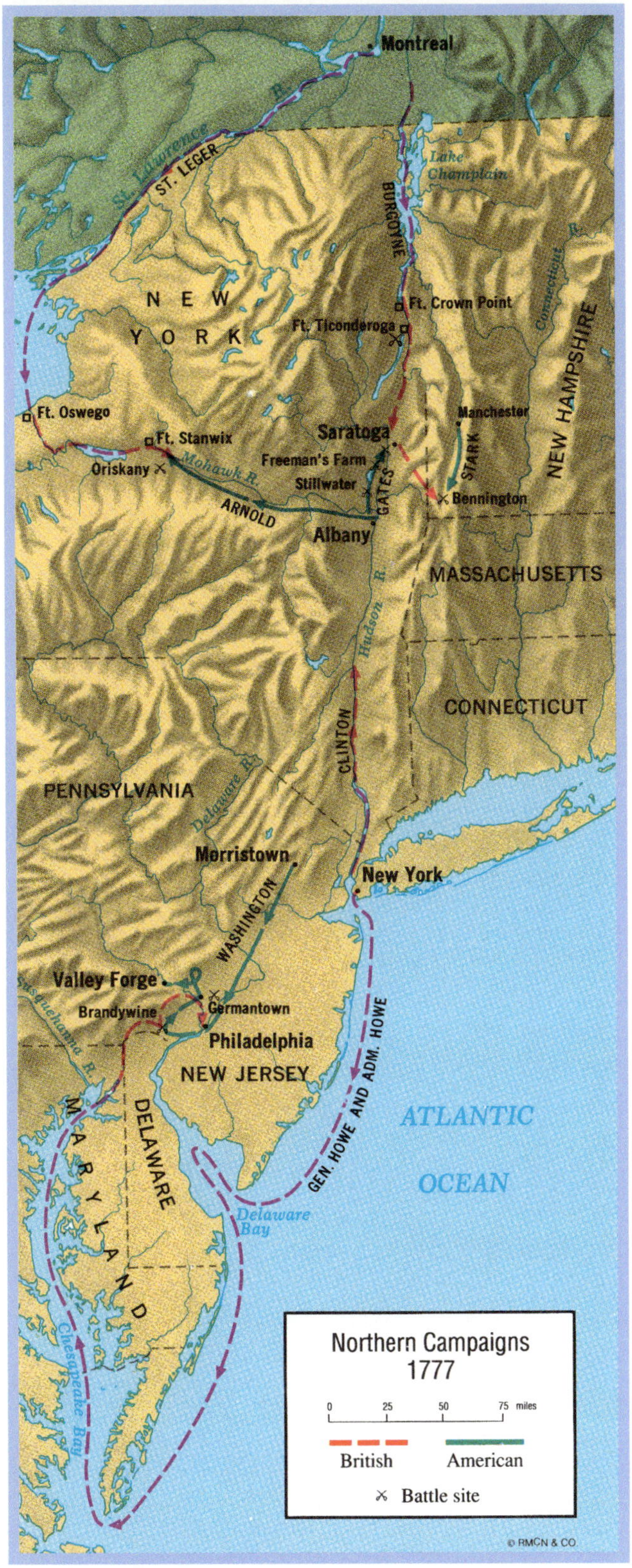

Americans suffered heavy losses at Philadelphia and Germantown, but their victory at Saratoga convinced France to enter the war on the American side. a

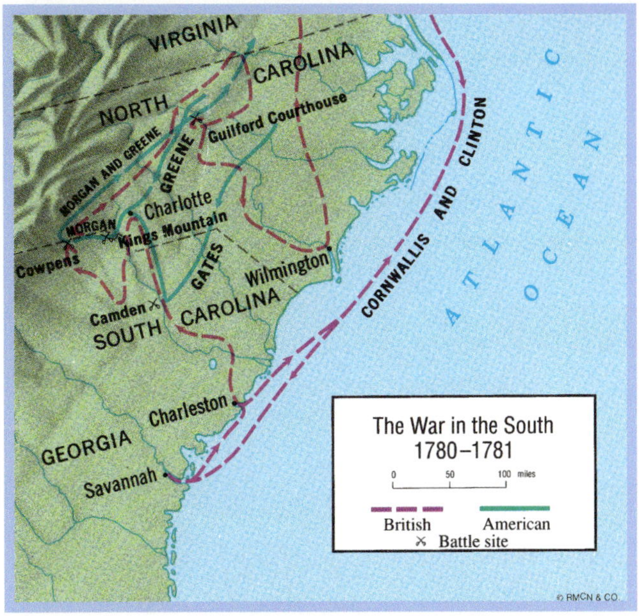

British troops sailed to major ports in the South. b

The war ended at Yorktown when General Charles Cornwallis and his troops surrendered. c

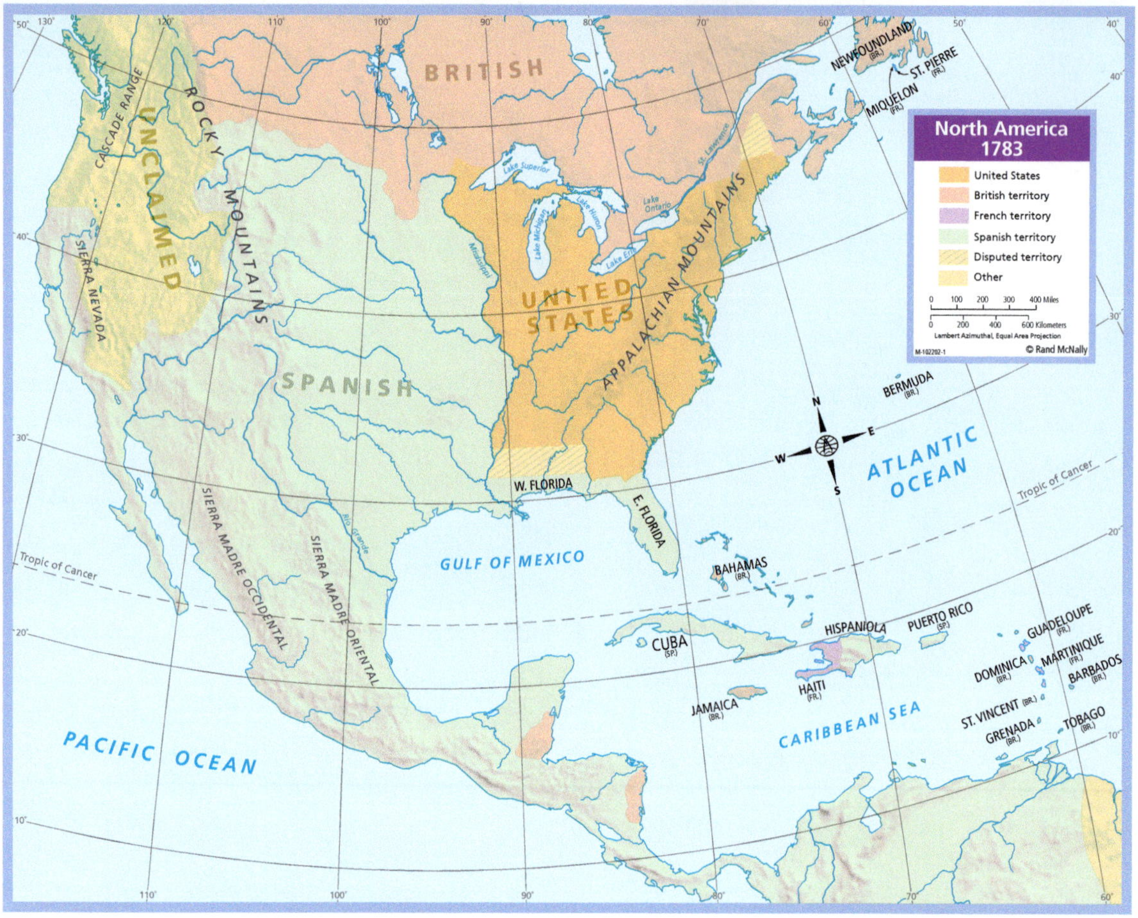

a

▲ The Treaty of Paris of 1783 established the boundaries of the United States. The new nation extended from the Atlantic Ocean to the Mississippi River and from 31° north latitude to the Canadian border. The treaty granted Florida to Spain.

b

▲ The Spanish established forts to protect their lands and missions to spread their faith.

▲ States with western land claims were asked to put the good of the country above their own interests. Virginia was first to give up its claims. By 1802 all states had ceded their western lands to the United States.

a

▲ Increasing numbers of Americans settled west of the Appalachians. Kentucky and Tennessee became states. Great Britain and Spain disputed areas of land added to the United States in 1783.

b

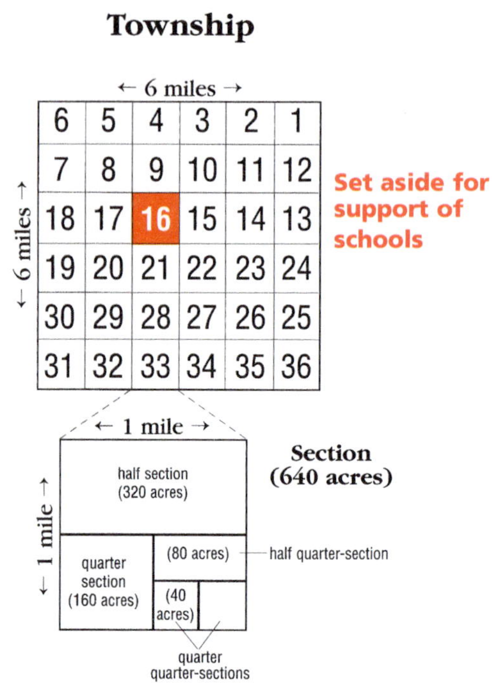

▲ The Northwest Territory was land north of the Ohio River that later became the states of Ohio, Indiana, Illinois, Michigan, and Wisconsin. The Land Ordinance of 1785 provided a plan for the sale of this land.

Public lands were divided into townships that were six miles square. Each township was divided into 36 sections, as shown on the diagram. Each section consisted of 640 acres, and it sold for $1 per acre. The small white square in the grid on the map represents one township.

In the 1780s, few settlers could afford to buy a section of land. Companies such as the Ohio Company and Scioto Company bought land from the government and divided it into smaller lots. Then they sold it to settlers at a profit.

Section 16 in each township was set aside by the government for the support of education. Settlers could rent or sell this land to raise money for public schools.

Section 4 | (1790-1870)

The Gateway Arch stands along the Mississippi River in St. Louis. It honors the Louisiana Purchase and the pioneers who settled the West.

This monument marks the Oregon Trail, which thousands of pioneers traveled from Independence, Missouri, to the Oregon Country.

Between 1790 and 1870, the United States expanded its boundaries to the Pacific coast. Through the Louisiana Purchase in 1803, it acquired the vast land between the Mississippi River and the Rocky Mountains. Through war with Mexico, 1846-1848, it gained land in the Southwest. Through a treaty with Britain in 1846, it gained land in the Pacific Northwest. Within 70 years after the United States became an independent nation, it had tripled in size.

Explorers, trappers, and traders blazed trails to the West. Pioneers rapidly settled new territories, pushing the **frontier**, or edge of settled land, west of the Mississippi River. Settlers followed the Oregon Trail to the Pacific Northwest. Mormons traveled to Utah in search of religious freedom. Gold seekers poured into California. Millions of immigrants from Europe came to the United States seeking a better life.

Did You Know

Francis Scott Key wrote "The Star-Spangled Banner" during the War of 1812 as he watched the bombardment of Fort McHenry from a ship in Baltimore Harbor. The words were set to music and later became our national anthem.

Area of Selected Lands Added to the United States, 1803-1867

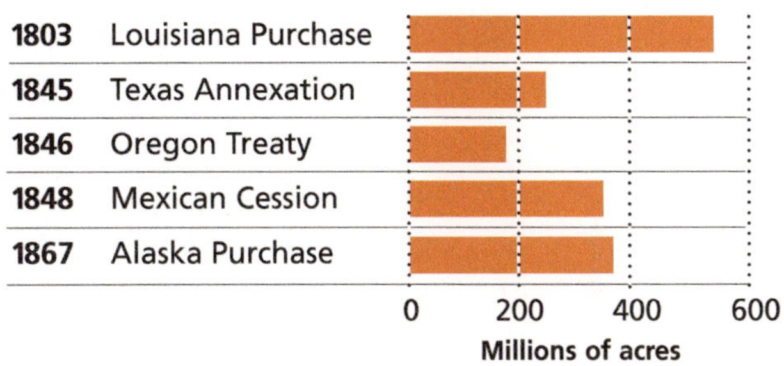

People

- **1803** President Thomas Jefferson purchases Louisiana Territory from France.
- **1847** Brigham Young leads Mormon migration from Illinois to the Great Salt Lake.
- **1848** Elizabeth Cady Stanton and Lucretia Mott hold women's rights convention in New York.

Events

- **1819** United States acquires Florida from Spain.
- **1825** Erie Canal links the Great Lakes and Atlantic Ocean.
- **1849** Gold rush brings thousands of people to California.

Literature

- **1820** "Rip Van Winkle," by Washington Irving, is set in the Catskill Mountains.
- **1827** *The Prairie,* by James Fenimore Cooper, describes frontier life on the western plains.
- **1854** *Walden,* by Henry David Thoreau, describes the beauty of nature in Massachusetts.

a

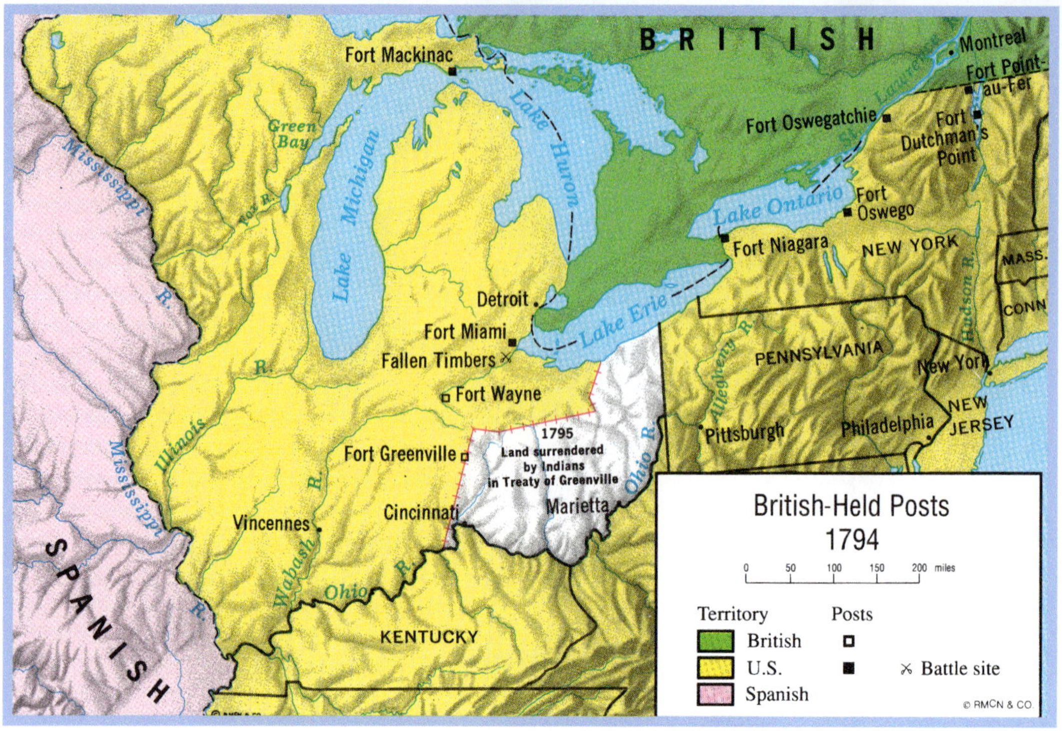

The British violated the Treaty of Paris of 1783 by keeping posts in U.S. territory.

b

Explorations of the Louisiana Purchase by Lewis and Clark and Pike provided valuable information about lands west of the Mississippi River.

a

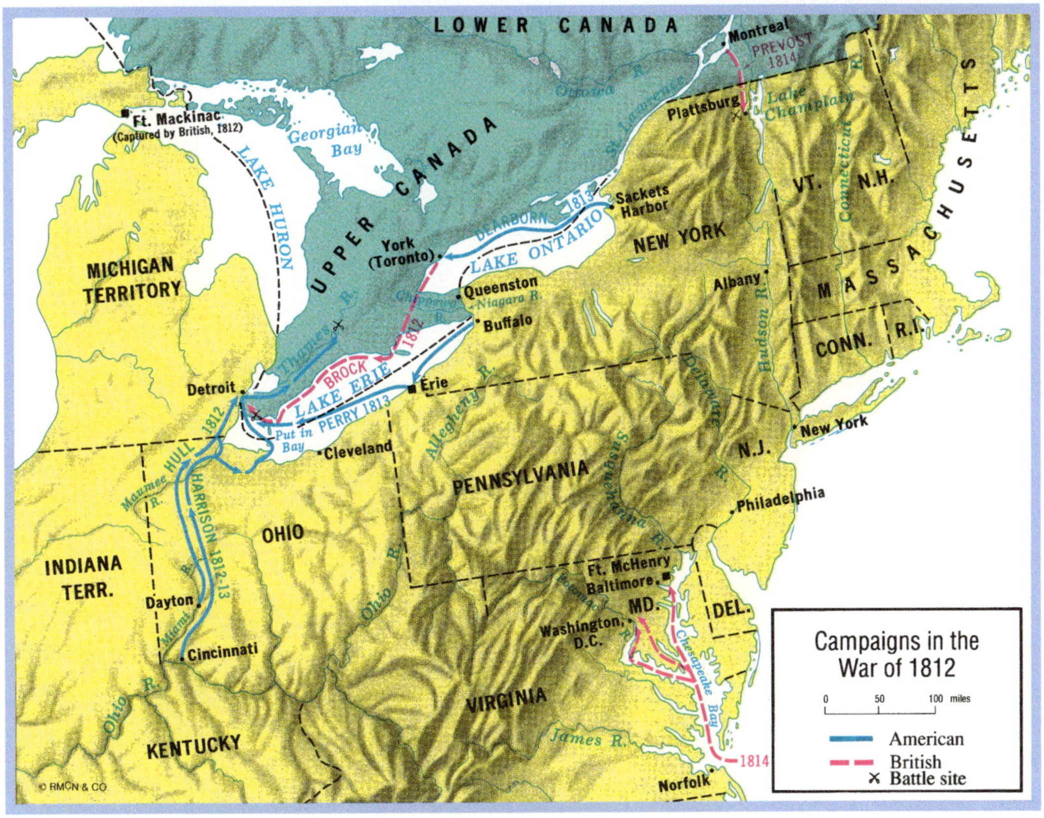

Campaigns in the War of 1812 were widely scattered. They included a decisive U.S. victory on Lake Erie as well as the British capture and burning of Washington, D.C.

b

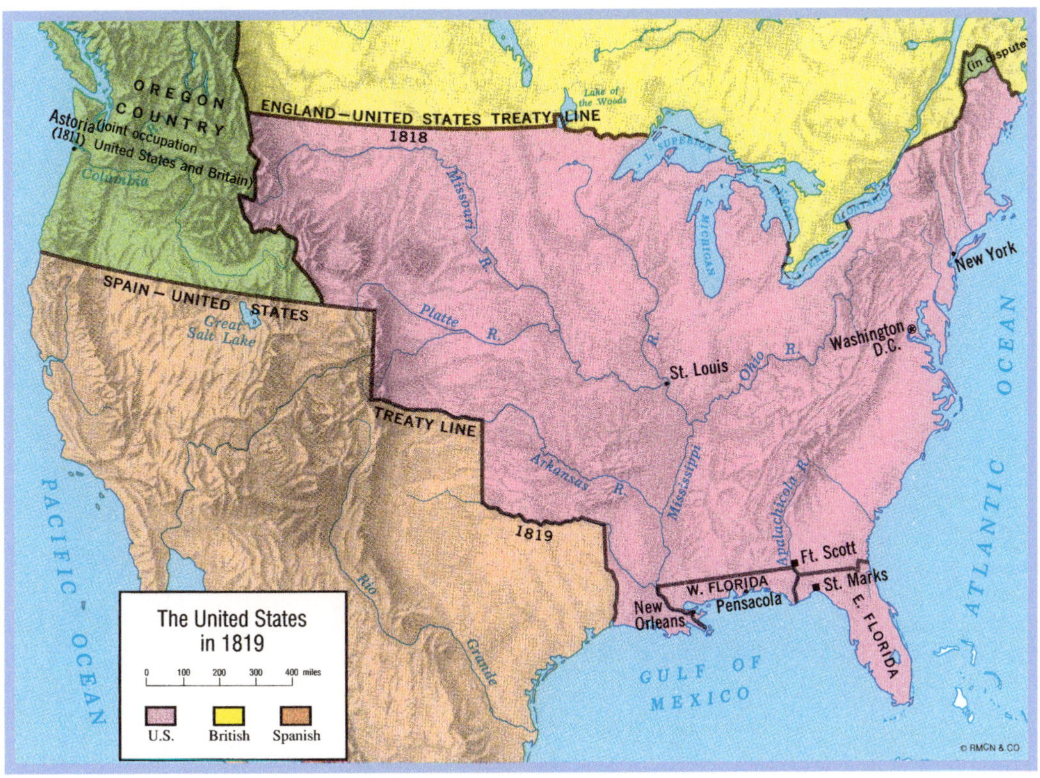

The Treaty of Ghent set a boundary between U.S. and British lands and allowed both nations to settle the Oregon Country. The Adams-Onis Treaty set a boundary between U.S. and Spanish lands and gave Florida to the United States.

a

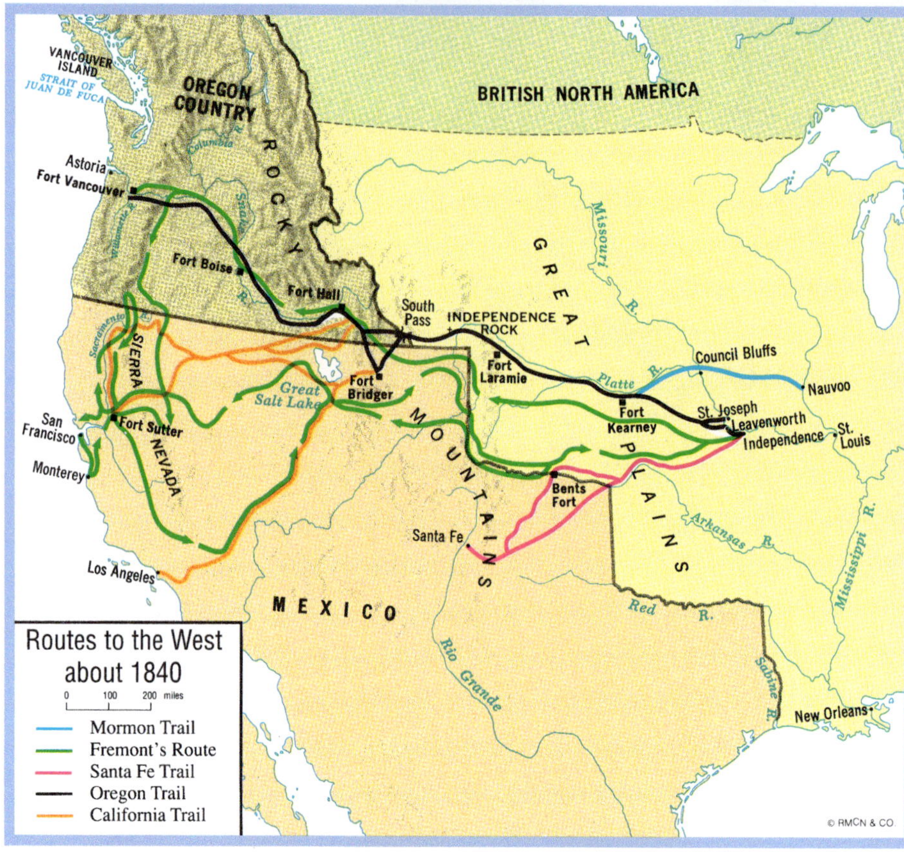

The constant traffic of settlers to the Oregon Country marked a trail across the Great Plains and Rocky Mountains. Traders and trappers blazed other trails that settlers later followed to the Far West.

b

The Mexican War began with a dispute over the southern boundary of Texas—the area shown in pink on the map. It ended when General Winfield Scott defeated Santa Anna and captured Mexico City. As a result of this war, the United States gained a large territory in the Southwest.

▲ The Cumberland Road, also called the National Road, extended from Maryland to Illinois. The Erie Canal provided a link between the Great Lakes and the Atlantic Ocean.

a

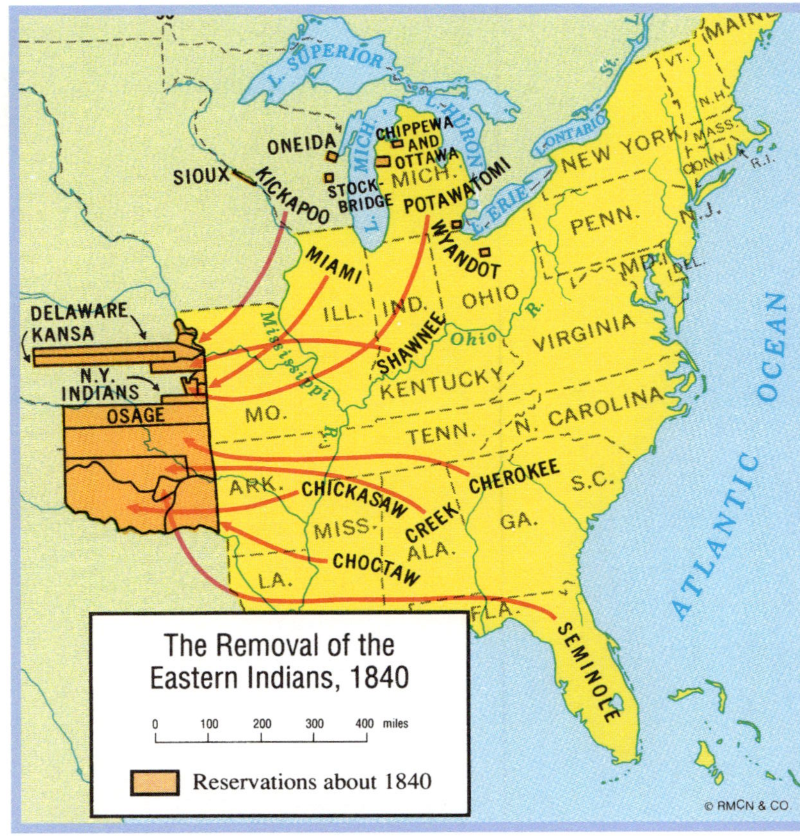

▲ The U.S. government forced Native Americans to leave their lands in the East and move to reservations in the West. The journey of 15,000 Cherokees from Georgia to Oklahoma became known as the Trail of Tears. About 4,000 Native Americans died along the way.

b

Between 1800 and 1850, the United States added fifteen new states and extended its borders to the Pacific Coast.

By 1850 settlement had spread west of the Mississippi River. Thousands of settlers also moved to the Far West.

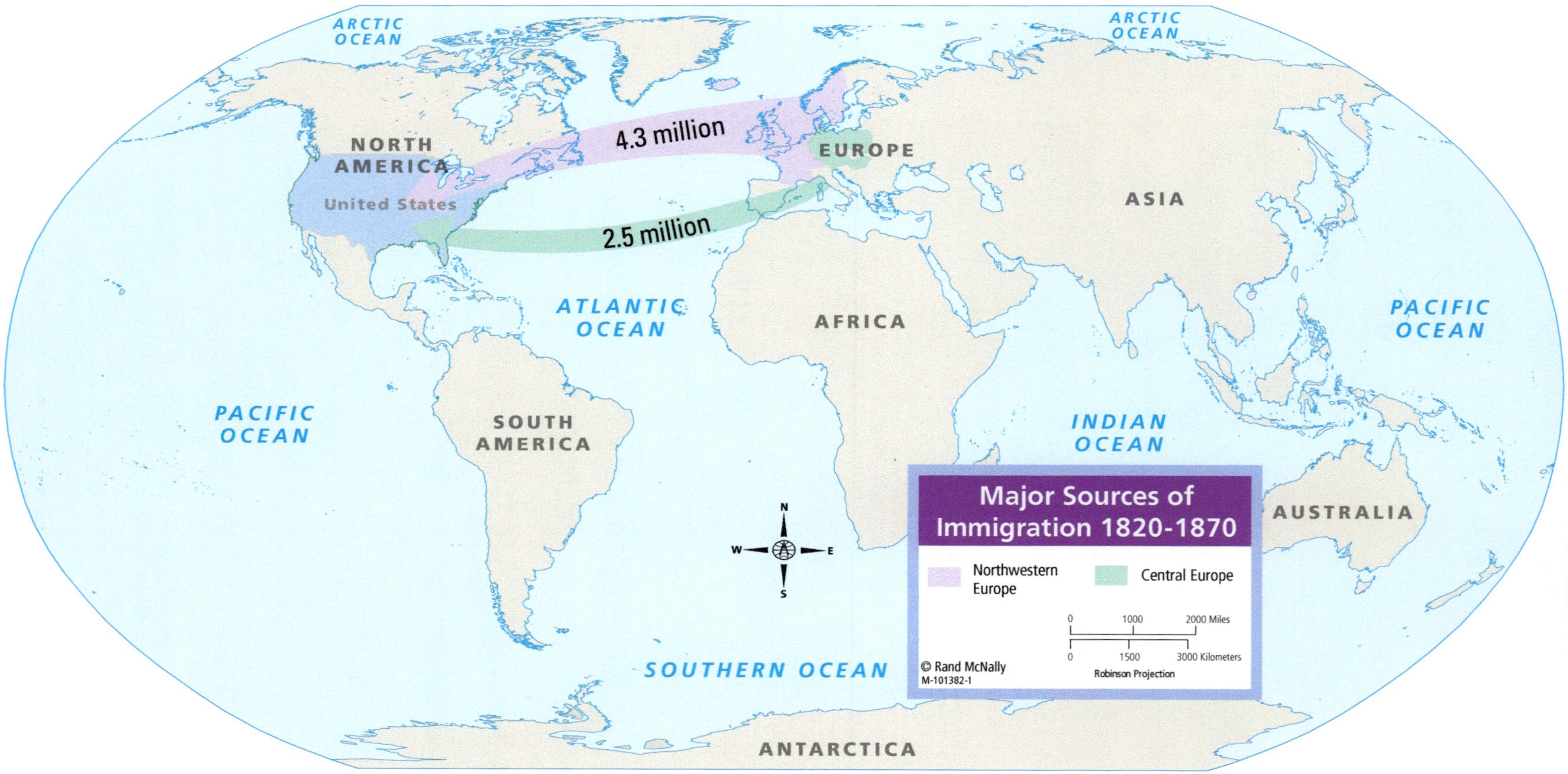

▲ Between 1820 and 1870, about 7.5 million immigrants came to the United States. Most came from northern and western Europe. Crop failure and poverty led Irish, German, and Scandinavian immigrants to see a better life in America.

Section 5 | (1850-1865)

The Battle of Gettysburg took place at this site in Pennsylvania in July 1863.

This memorial to Confederate leaders is carved on Stone Mountain near Atlanta, Georgia.

Between 1850 and 1860, differences between the North and the South widened. The agricultural economy of the South was based on slave labor. Many Northerners viewed slavery as wrong. **Abolitionists**, or people who demanded an end to slavery, operated the Underground Railroad to help slaves escape. The Compromise of 1850 and the Kansas-Nebraska Act attempted to settle the issue of slavery in the West.

When Abraham Lincoln was elected president in 1860, Southerners feared he would end slavery. Eleven southern states **seceded**, or withdrew, from the Union and formed the Confederacy. An attack on Fort Sumter in April 1861 marked the beginning of the Civil War. The war ended when Confederate general Robert E. Lee surrendered at Appomattox in April 1865.

The bitter war between the North and the South left lasting problems. Much of the South was destroyed. More Americans lost their lives in the Civil War than in any other war in which the United States has fought.

American Deaths in Major Wars

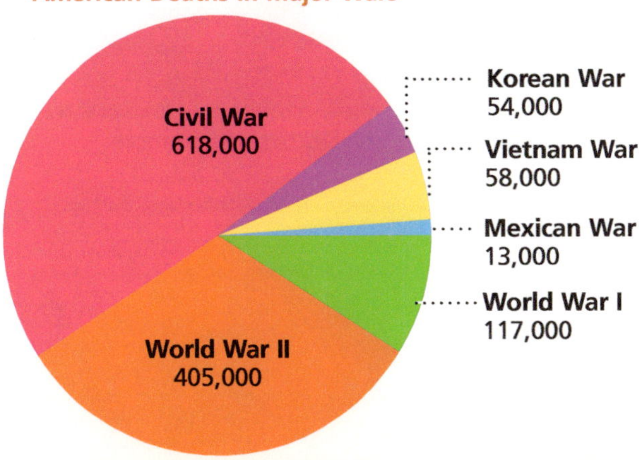

Did You Know

When Virginia seceded from the Union in 1861, 50 of its western counties separated from the state. These counties were admitted to the Union in 1863 as the state of West Virginia.

	1850	**1863**	**1865**
People	Harriet Tubman leads slaves from Maryland to freedom in the North.	Abraham Lincoln delivers Gettysburg Address on battlefield in Pennsylvania.	Robert E. Lee surrenders at Appomattox Court House, Virginia.
	1860	**1861**	**1865**
Events	South Carolina becomes first southern state to secede.	Civil War begins at Fort Sumter, South Carolina.	Thirteenth Amendment ends slavery in the United States.
	1850	**1852**	**1865**
Literature	*The Scarlet Letter*, by Nathaniel Hawthorne, is set in Puritan New England.	*Uncle Tom's Cabin*, by Harriet Beecher Stowe, highlights the cruelty of slavery in the South.	"Drum Taps," by Walt Whitman, describes scenes from Civil War battlefields.

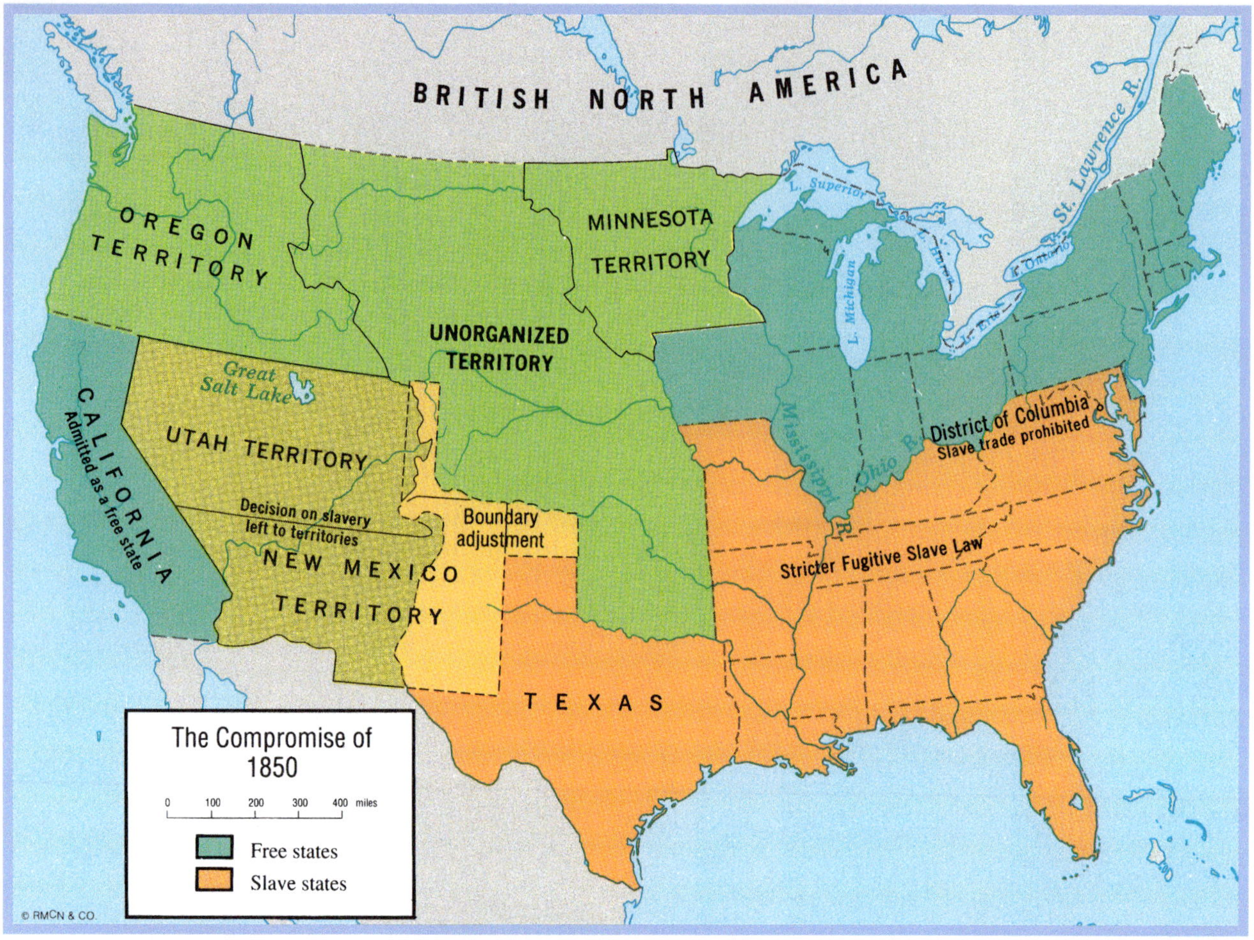

a

The Compromise of 1850 admitted California as a free state and ended slave trade in the District of Columbia. Utah and New Mexico Territories could decide the issue of slavery.

b

The Kansas-Nebraska Act allowed settlers in those territories to decide whether to allow slavery.

c

The Underground Railroad was a system of escape routes slaves followed to freedom.

Economic differences created different way of life in the North and South. Plantation crops, such as tobacco, cotton, and sugar cane, supported an agricultural economy based on slavery in the South. Advances in mass production and transportation supported an economy based on industry and trade in the North. Northern abolitionists viewed slavery as wrong and began a movement to end it.

The Confederate States of America consisted of eleven slave states that seceded from the Union between December 20, 1860 and May 20, 1861. The 24 remaining states, including West Virginia (which split from Virginia and became a state in 1863) and four other slave states, fought for the Union during the Civil War.

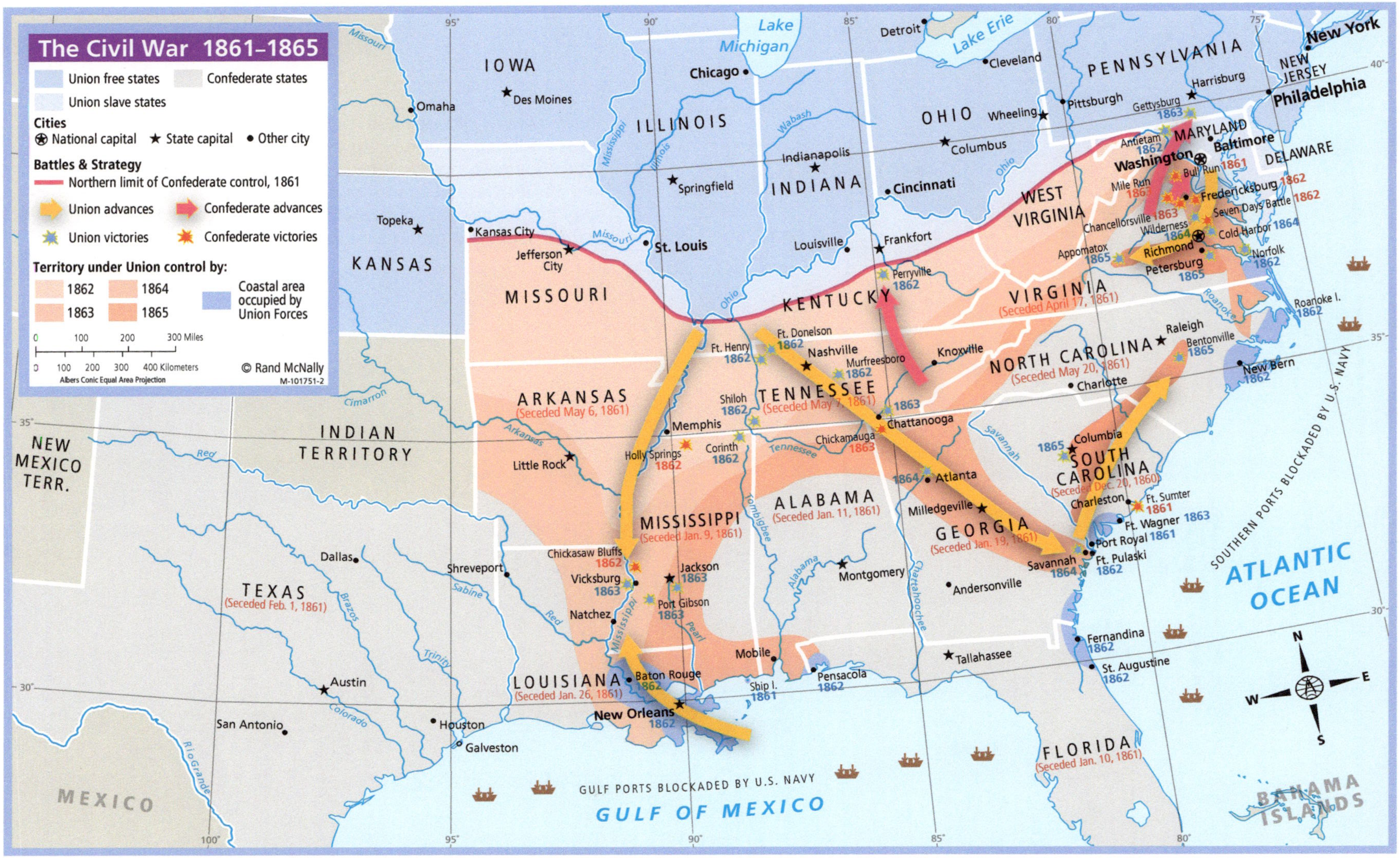

Most of the fighting in the East took place in Virginia. Much of the fighting in the West took place in Tennessee and along the Mississippi River. The map legend indicates how Union strategy succeeded by dividing the Confederacy and blockading its ports.

Union strategy involved blockading southern ports, splitting the Confederacy by gaining control of the Mississippi River Valley, and capturing Richmond. Confederate strategy involved defending the South from attack, breaking the Union blockade, and splitting the Union by gaining control of Washington, D.C., Maryland, and central Pennsylvania.

The Civil War 1861–1865

- Union victory
- Confederate victory
- Battle indecisive
- Union forces
- Confederate forces

Section 6 | (1860-1920)

This statue of Buffalo Bill Cody in Wyoming represents the Old West.

The Statue of Liberty in New York Harbor has welcomed immigrants since 1886. It was a gift to the United States from France.

The years between 1860 and 1920 included the end of one era in American history and the beginning of another. The Great Plains opened to settlers as the U.S. Army defeated the Plains Indians and forced them onto reservations. Texas cattle ranchers drove their herds to railroads, which provided transportation to eastern markets. **Homesteaders**, or settlers who received free land from the government in exchange for farming it, moved to western territories. By 1890, the long process of settling the United States from coast to coast was complete. The American frontier had come to an end.

In the late 1800s, the United States began to emerge as a modern nation. Millions of immigrants came from Europe to farm the land or work in factories. The United States became an industrial nation and acquired territories overseas. It purchased Alaska and established naval bases on islands in the Pacific. It fought a war with Spain by which it acquired additional territories. The United States entered World War I in 1917 and assumed its role as a world power.

Immigration to the United States, 1860-1919

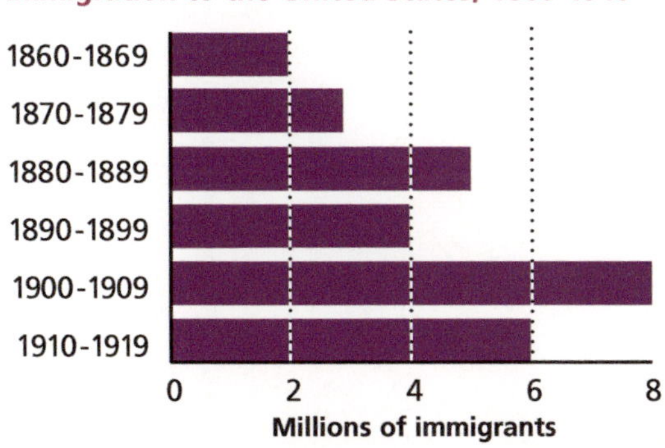

Did You Know

In 1850 about 20 million bison, or buffaloes, roamed the Great Plains. The westward movement almost wiped out these animals. By 1890, only about 500 bison could be found in the West.

	1877	**1889**	**1898**
People	Chief Joseph leads Nez Percés on a retreat through Idaho and Montana.	Jane Addams opens Hull House to help immigrants in Chicago.	Theodore Roosevelt leads Rough Riders in Cuba during Spanish-American War.
	1867	**1892**	**1898**
Events	United States purchases Alaska from Russia.	Ellis Island, in New York Harbor, becomes an immigration station.	Hawaii becomes a U.S. territory.
	1876	**1881**	**1912**
Literature	*The Adventures of Tom Sawyer*, by Mark Twain, is set in Hannibal, Missouri.	A Century of Dishonor, by Helen Hunt Jackson, describes mistreatment of Native Americans in the U.S.	*Riders of the Purple Sage*, by Zane Grey, describes life in the West.

▲ After 1860, the population west of the Mississippi River grew rapidly. Native Americans lost the battle to keep their lands, and the government moved them to reservations. Ranchers and farmers spread settlement throughout the Great Plains and the Far West. Although large areas of the West remained thinly populated, in 1890 the Census Bureau declared the frontier had come to an end.

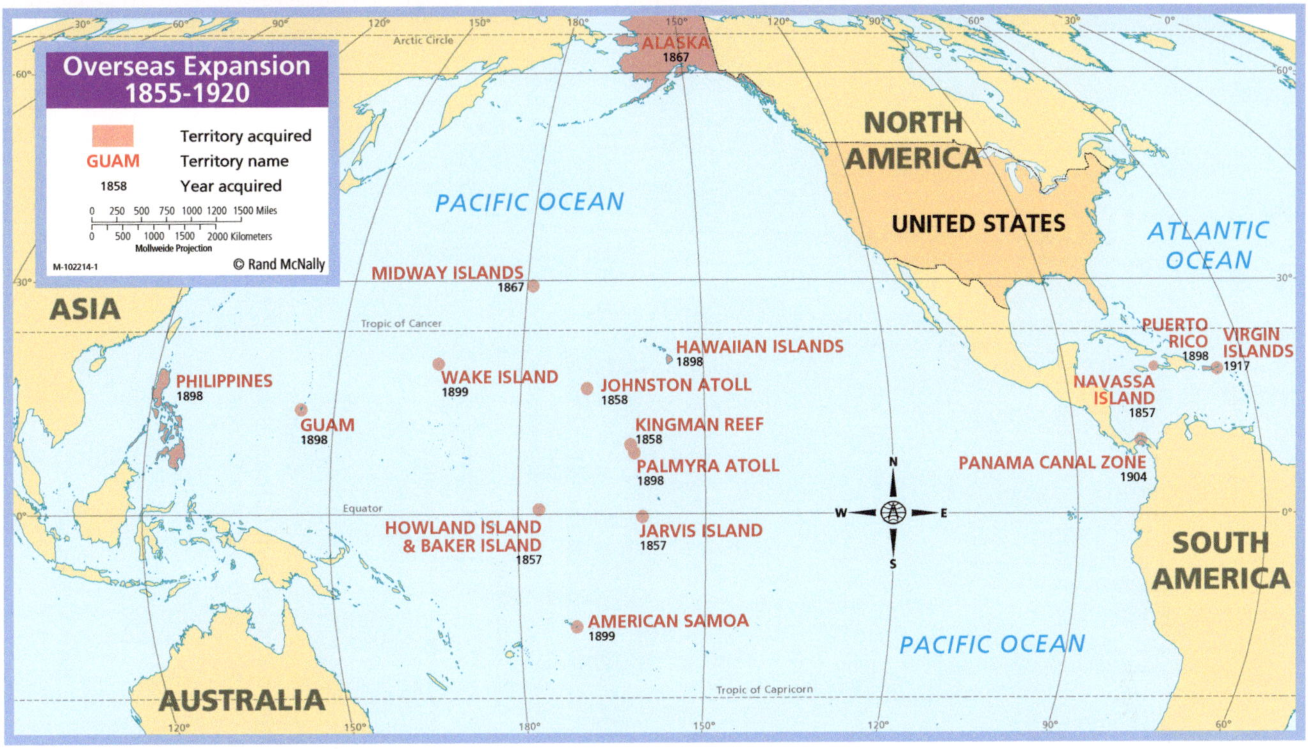

a

▲The United States acquired islands in the Pacific Ocean that served as fueling stations for ships traveling to and from China and Japan. The Hawaiian Islands also provided raw materials for import or trade.

b

▲In the Battle of Manila Bay, American ships commanded by Commodore George Dewey destroyed the Spanish fleet in the Philippines.

c

▲The sinking of the American battleship Maine in Havana harbor brought the United States into war with Spain. The war was fought in both Cuba and the Philippines. As a result of the Spanish-American War, Spain granted freedom to Cuba and ceded Guam, Puerto Rico, and the Philippines to the United States.

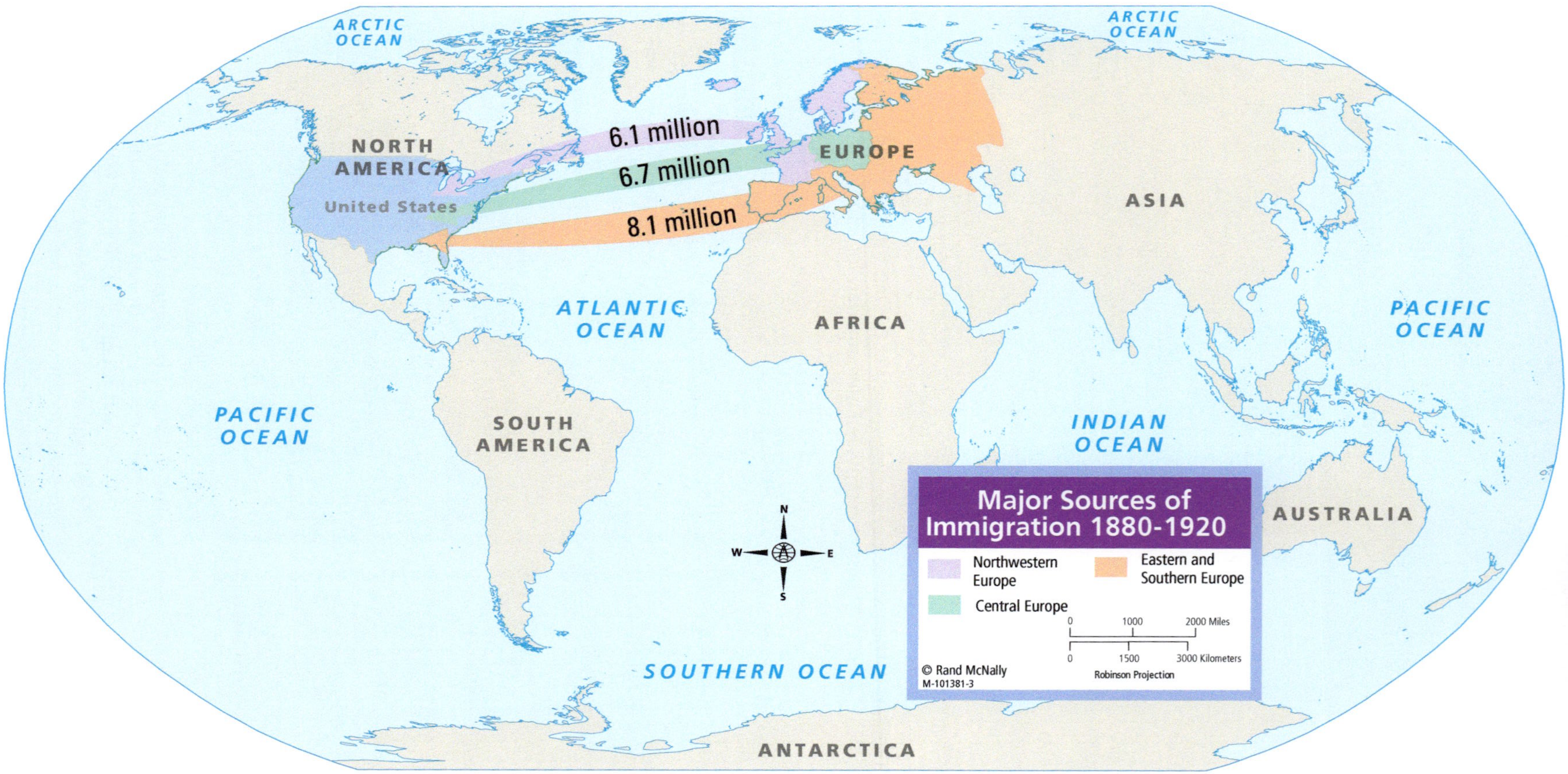

▲ Between 1880 and 1920, more than 20 million immigrants came to the United States. Unlike earlier newcomers, who came mostly from northern and western Europe, these so-called "new immigrants" came mostly from central, eastern, and southern Europe.

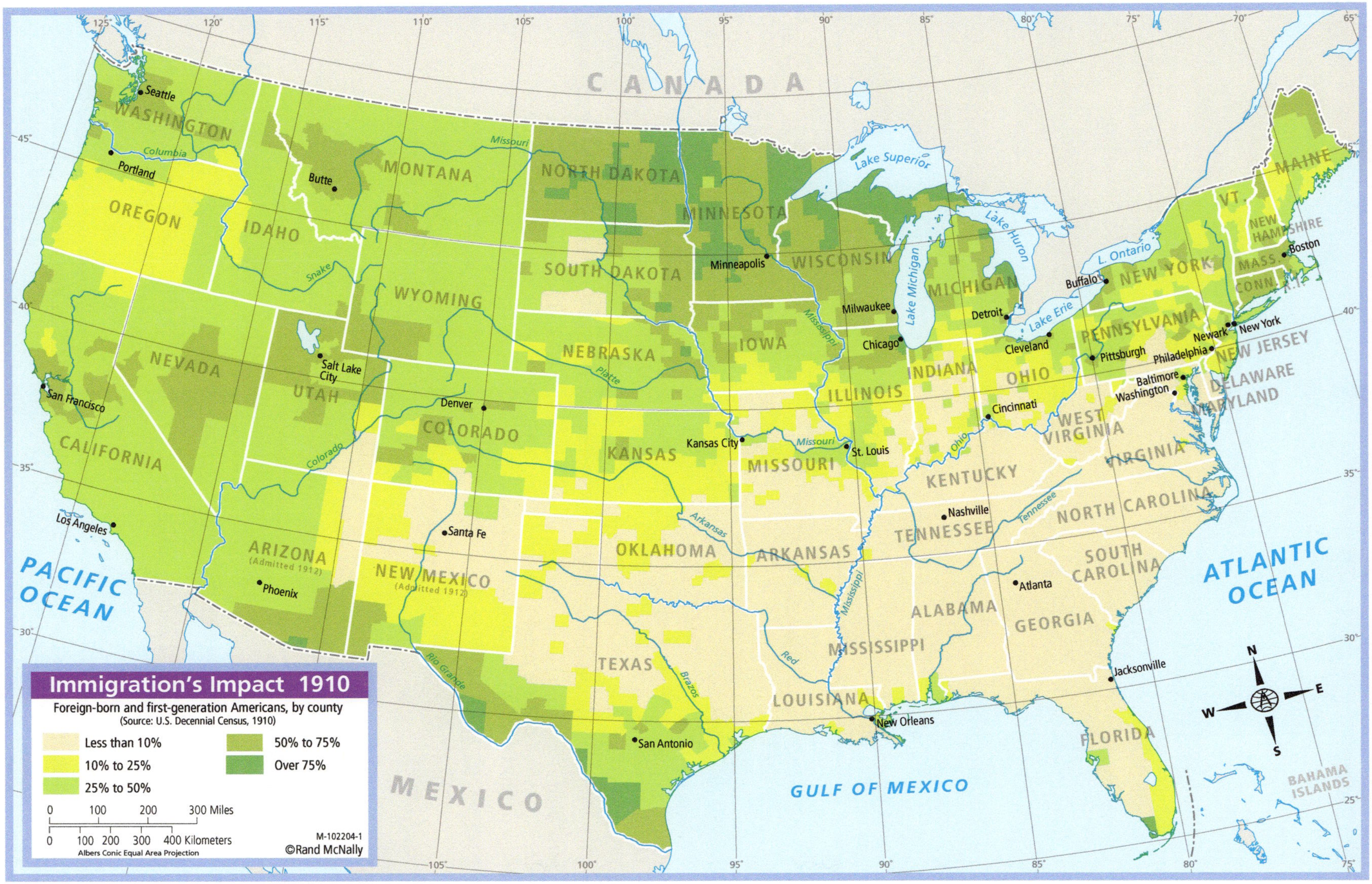

Many immigrants settled in large cities in the East. Mining attracted newcomers to Montana, Colorado, and Nevada. Railroad companies encouraged European workers to settle in the West. Poor economic conditions in Mexico led thousands of immigrants to settle in the United States.

In 1914, long-standing problems in Europe erupted in war between the Allied Powers and the Central Powers. The conflict, which became known as World War I, lasted four years. It involved more countries and caused more destruction than had any previous war. **a**

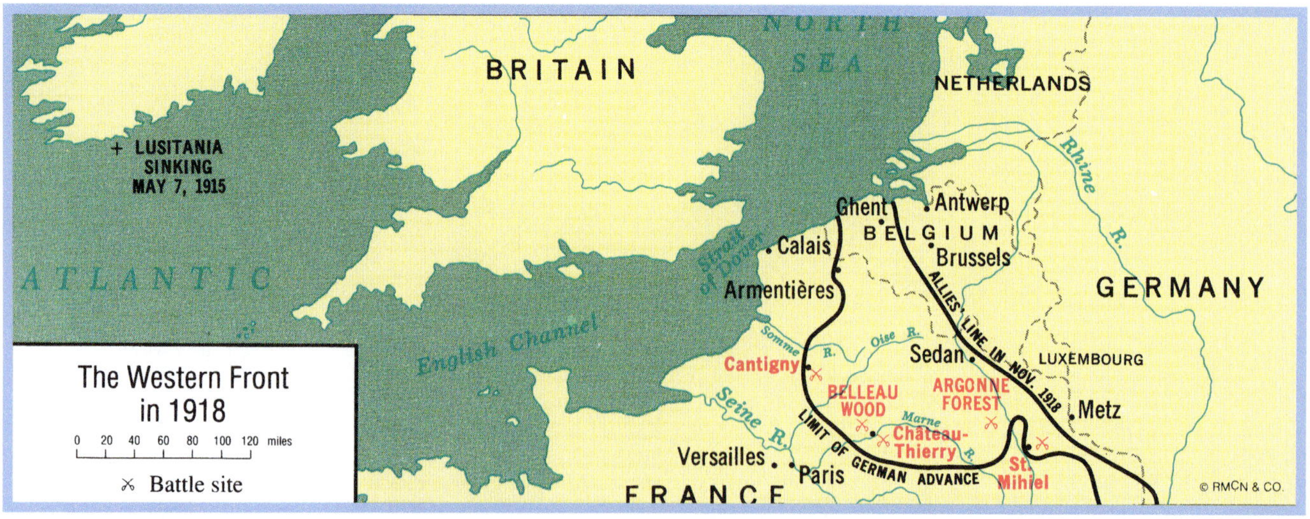

The loss of American lives abroad the Lusitania helped draw the United States into the war in Europe. American troops helped the Allies defeat the Germans on the Western Front, which stretched through Belgium and France. **b**

Challenges & Changes in the 20th Century

Section 7 | (1920-1999)

The United States Marine Corps Memorial in Arlington, Virginia, honors the flag raising on Iwo Jima during World War II.

In 1940 Houston, Texas, ranked 21st in population among U.S. cities. By 1999, it was the nation's tenth-largest metropolitan area.

During the decades between 1920 and 1999, the United States faced many challenges and experienced many changes. The economic prosperity of the 1920s ended with the stock market crash in 1929. Poverty and unemployment were widespread during the Great Depression of the 1930s. During World War II (1941-1945), United States troops fought in Europe and in the Pacific. After this war, the United States and the Soviet Union emerged as the world's leading powers.

The struggle between the Communist world, led by the Soviet Union, and the Democratic/Capitalist world, led by the United States, was called the **Cold War**. Between 1950 and 1990, the United States intervened in Korea, in Southeast Asia, and in Central America and the Caribbean to stop the spread of communism. The Cold War ended in 1991 when the Soviet Union was dissolved.

Changes took place within the United States as Americans moved from one area of the country to another, and suburbs grew around major cities. The **gross domestic product** (GDP), or value of all goods and services produced within the country, rose dramatically from the 1940s into the 1990s.

Gross Domestic Product, 1920-1999

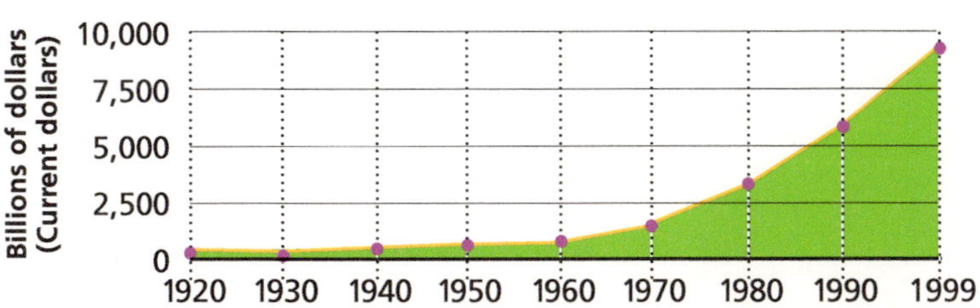

Did You Know

Between 1941 and 1945, one in every five Americans moved from one part of the United States to another.

People	**1927** Charles Lindbergh makes first nonstop flight from New York to Paris.	**1963** Dr. Martin Luther King, Jr., leads civil rights march on Washington, D.C.	**1981** Arizona judge Sandra Day O'Connor becomes first woman to serve on the Supreme Court.
Events	**1959** Alaska and Hawaii become states.	**1969** American astronauts walk on the moon.	**1991** The Cold War ends when the Soviet Union breaks into 15 independent republics.
Literature	**1939** *The Grapes of Wrath*, by John Steinbeck, tells of an Oklahoma family during the Great Depression.	**1961** *To Kill a Mockingbird*, by Harper Lee, explores racial prejudice in Alabama.	**1991** *The Lost Garden*, by Lawrence Yep, describes how the author grew up as a Chinese American in San Francisco.

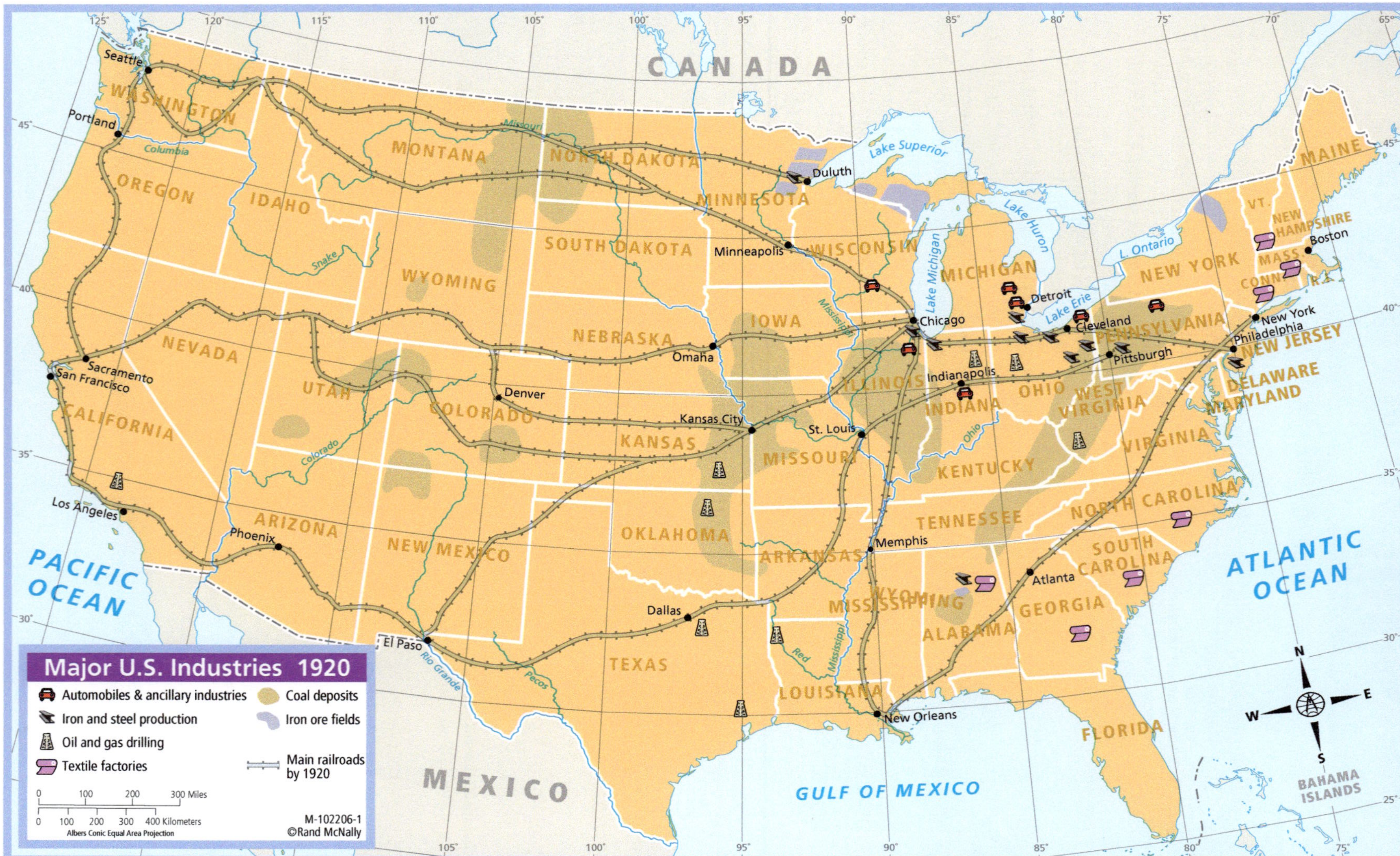

By 1920 the United States was a leading industrial nation. Advances in technology enabled workers to produce more goods faster. The demand for petroleum and steel increased to meet the growing needs of new industries such as the automobile industry. Spectacular economic growth provided a high standard of living for many Americans.

▲ Economic prosperity ended abruptly when the stock market crashed in 1929. The United States suffered through the Great Depression for the next 10 years. Millions of workers lost their jobs. Severe drought on the Great Plains contributed to dust storms that forced thousands of farmers to abandon their land.

World War II began in 1939 when Germany, under Nazi dictator Adolf Hitler, invaded Poland. The Axis Powers (Germany, Italy, Japan, and their partners) fought against the Allied Powers (shown in gold on the map). Belligerents were countries that fought in the war. Few nations remained neutral. By 1942, the Axis controlled most of Europe, northern Africa, and parts of Asia and the Pacific Ocean. German submarines attacked Allied cargo ships in the Atlantic.

The Japanese attack on Pearl Harbor, Hawaii, in December 1941 brought the United States into the war. American troops and supplies were sent to Europe and to the Pacific. The map indicated transportation time by air and by water from the United States to selected sites. During 1942, Allied forces halted Axis expansion in northern Africa, the Soviet Union, and the Pacific.

World War II
The Height of Axis Expansion
1942

- Territory controlled by Axis (Germany, Italy, Japan) late 1942
- 1941 — Areas of German submarine concentration
- Belligerents against Axis, late 1942. Also France, Poland, Norway, Netherlands, Belgium, Luxembourg, Greece, Yugoslavia, Philippine Commonwealth at war with Axis, before 1942. North African and Latin American countries, 1943–1945.
- × Battles
- 9 days — Days of ship time from the U.S.A.
- 20 hours — Hours of air time from the U.S.A.
- Political boundaries as of 1938

In 1943 and 1944, the Allies captured Japanese-held islands in the Pacific. In August 1945, the United States dropped an atomic bomb on Hiroshima, Japan. World War II ended when the Japanese surrendered in September 1945.

▲ After defeating the Axis in northern Africa, the Allies focused on Europe. Italy surrendered in 1943. In 1944 Allies landed in northern France and advanced on Germany from the west, while Soviet troops advanced from the east. Germany surrendered in May 1945.

In 1949 the United States and other free nations formed a military alliance called the North Atlantic Treaty Organization (NATO) to prevent the spread of communism. The Soviet Union and other Communist countries formed a competing alliance called the Warsaw Pact. This view indicates why Canada and the United States feared a possible Soviet attack from the north.

a

▲ United Nations members, including the United States, sent troops to defend South Korea from an invasion by Communist-rules North Korea. In 1950, UN forces halted the North Korean advance at Pusan and pushed to the Yalu River in the north. The war ended in 1953 when the UN and North Korea signed an armistice agreement.

b

▲ The Vietnam War began in 1957. Starting in the 1960s, the United States began sending combat troops to the region to prevent Communist-ruled North Vietnam from taking over non-Communist South Vietnam. The Ho Chi Minh Trail was a system of roads the North Vietnamese used as a supply route for the Viet Cong, or Communist rebels in South Vietnam.

Between 1940 and 1970, millions of African Americans moved out of the South. More than two-thirds of the total African American population relocated to cities. More than half the urban black population was concentrated in the twelve cities shown on the map.

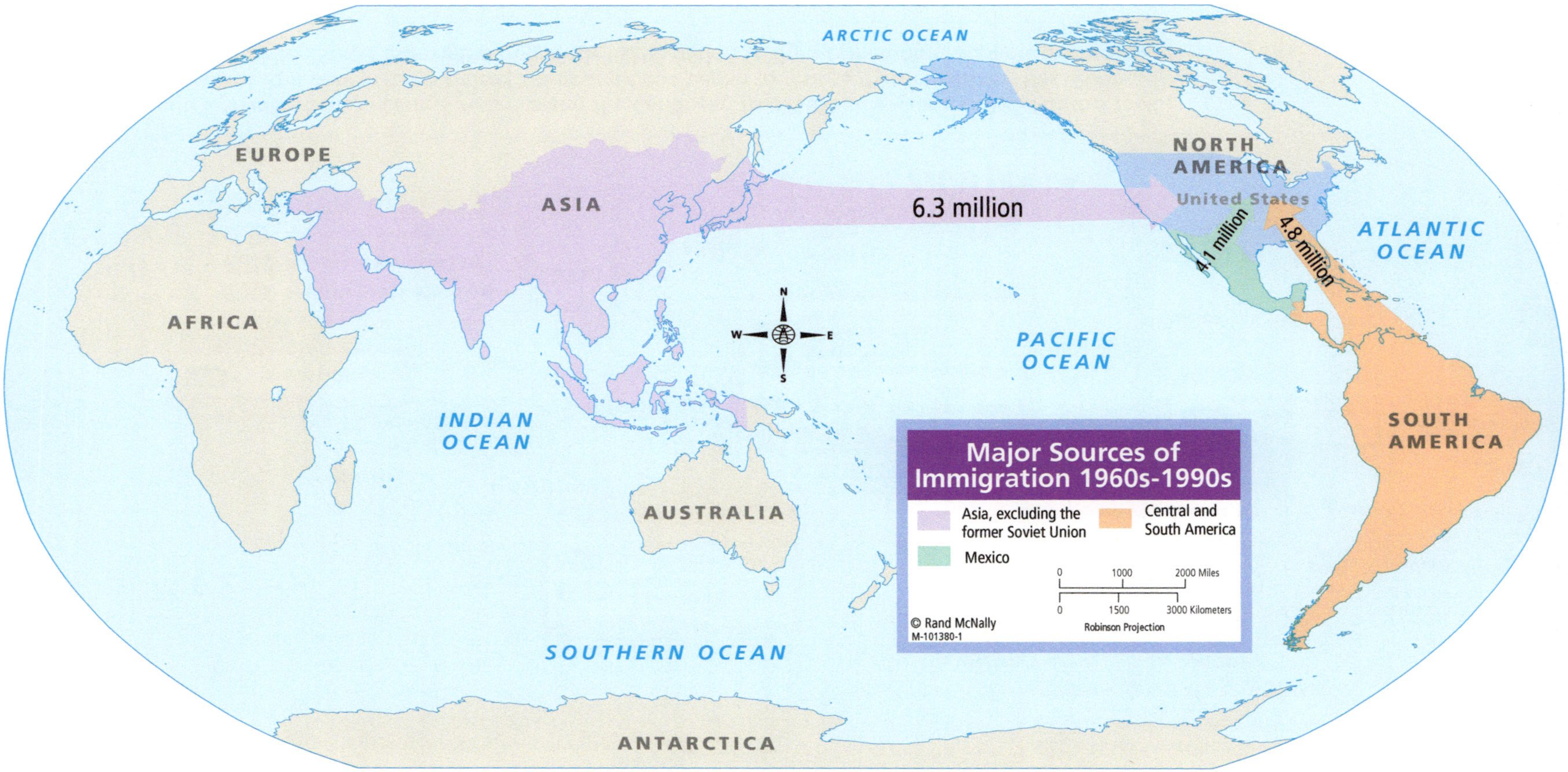

Changes in U.S. immigration laws in the 1960s changed immigration patterns. Percentages of immigrants from Europe decreased. In the 1990s, most immigrants to the United States came from Mexico, the Philippines, Haiti, China, India, Vietnam, Jamaica, Cuba, and South Korea.

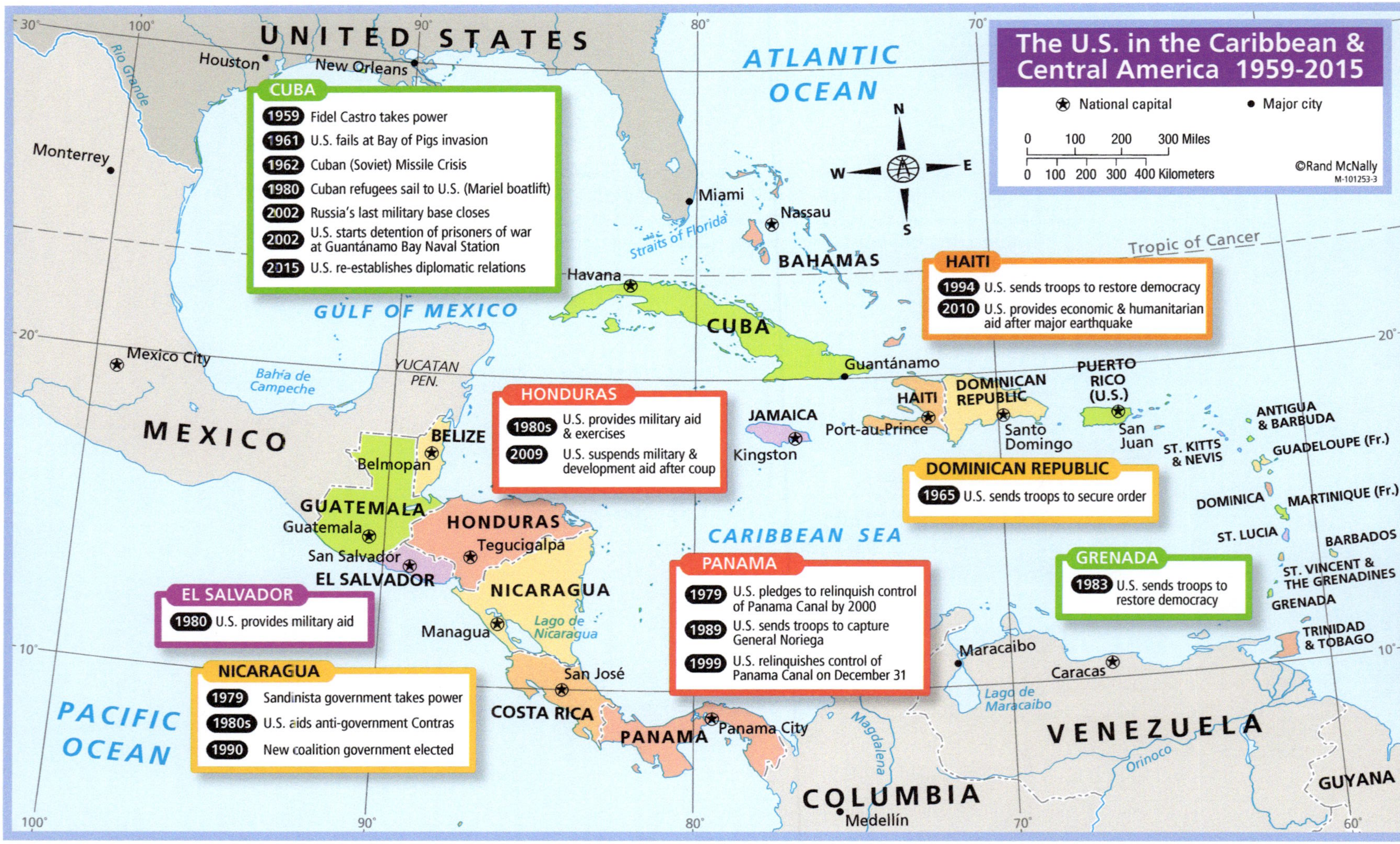

This map traces U.S. involvement in Central America and the Caribbean from 1959, the year that Fidel Castro took power in Cuba, to 2015, the year that the United States and Cuba began to restore their diplomatic ties. During these six decades, the United States intervened frequently in the region to fight communism, support democracy, and protect U.S. interests.

Entering a New Millennium

Section 8 | (2000 & beyond)

Skyscrapers tower over midtown Manhattan in New York—the largest U.S. city in population in 2020. One World Trade Center tower, which opened in 2014, is the tallest building in the Western Hemisphere.

After a deadly hurricane hit New Orleans in 2005, city residents worked together to rebuild their communities.

In 2000 the United States entered a new millennium as one of the world's leading nations. Its principles of freedom and opportunity provided its people with one of the world's highest standards of living. The advent of the Internet made it easy to exchange ideas and information quickly.

The diverse population of the United States reflected the history of a nation settled by people from every part of the world. By the time of the 2000 census, most Americans lived in large metropolitan areas, or cities surrounded by suburbs. They lived longer and were better educated than Americans in the past.

Yet the new millennium also brought new challenges for the United States and the world. Americans showed courage and resolve in response to terrorist attacks on New York City, Boston, and Washington, D.C. Wars in Afghanistan and Iraq tested U.S. military strength and resources. Starting in 2008, a worldwide financial crisis threatened economic gains. Protecting human rights, defending national security, and supporting economic development remain key issues for the nation.

Population Distribution by Age, 1910 and 2020

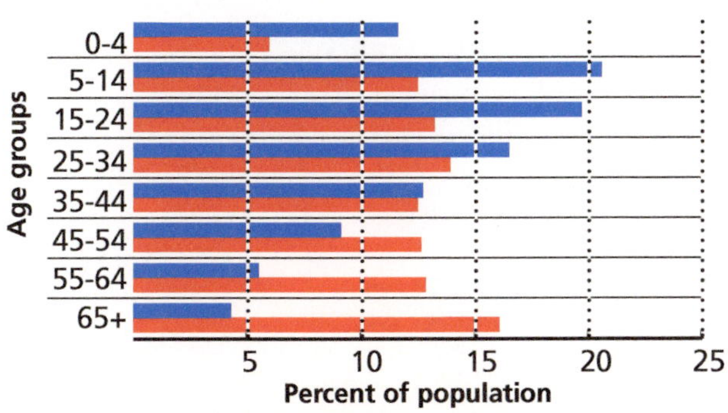

Did You Know

The Miami, Florida, metropolitan area has the largest concentration of immigrants in the country. More than one-third of its residents moved there from other countries.

	2002	**2007**	**2009**
People	Ellen Ochoa, co-inventor of optical analysis systems and the first Hispanic female astronaut, makes her fourth voyage on the space shuttle.	Former vice president Al Gore receives the Nobel Peace Prize for his efforts to raise awareness about global warming.	Barack Obama becomes the first African American president of the United States.
	2001	**2010**	**2020**
Events	Terrorists attack the World Trade center and the Pentagon on September 11. In response, U.S.-led forces attack Afghanistan.	An oil rig explosion in the Gulf of Mexico causes the worst oil spill in U.S. history.	Over 100 million Americans infected with Coronavirus during COVID-19 pandemic.
	2001	**2002**	**2008**
Literature	*Pleasure Dome*, a collection of poems by Yusef Komunyakaa, explores such topics as his Southern roots, his experiences in Vietnam, and jazz music.	*A Song Flung Up to Heaven*, by Maya Angelou, completes the autobiography of the African American poet.	*The Brief Wondrous Life of Oscar Wao*, by Junot Díaz, tells the story of a family of Dominican immigrants in the United States.

B.C.
ALBERTA
SASKATCHEWAN
MANITOBA
WASHINGTON
OREGON
IDAHO
MONTANA
WYOMING
NORTH DAKOTA
SOUTH DAKOTA
NEBRASKA
NEVADA
UTAH
COLORADO
KANSAS
CALIFORNIA
ARIZONA
NEW MEXICO
OKLAHOMA
TEXAS
MEXICO
PACIFIC OCEAN
ROCKY MOUNTAINS
CASCADE RANGE
SIERRA NEVADA
COAST RANGES
GREAT BASIN
WASATCH RANGE
BITTERROOT RANGE
SALMON RIVER MOUNTAINS
SACRAMENTO MTS.
BLACK HILLS
BADLANDS
Victoria
Bellingham
Everett
Seattle
Olympia
Tacoma
Mt. Olympus 7,969
Mt. Rainier 14,411
Mt. Saint Helens 8,364
Spokane
Yakima
Kennewick
Walla Walla
Longview
Portland
Salem
Mt. Hood 11,239
Corvallis
Eugene
Coos Bay
Cape Blanco
Bend
Pendleton
Baker City
Medford
Klamath Falls
Mt. McLoughlin 9,495
Coeur d'Alene
Moscow
Lewiston
Nampa
Boise
Twin Falls
Pocatello
Idaho Falls
Rexburg
Borah Peak 12,662
Salmon
Kalispell
Missoula
Butte
Helena
Great Falls
Bozeman
Billings
Havre
Miles City
Granite Peak 12,799
Cody
Sheridan
Francs Peak 13,153
Cloud Peak 13,167
Grand Teton 13,770
Casper
Rock Springs
Laramie
Cheyenne
Williston
Minot
Dickinson
Bismarck
Jamestown
Aberdeen
Spearfish
Rapid City
Black Elk Peak 7,242
Pierre
Mitchell
Scottsbluff
North Platte
Kearney
Grand Island
Hastings
Norfolk
Mt. Shasta 14,162
Eureka
Redding
Alturas
Chico
Winnemucca
Elko
Reno
Sparks
Carson City
Ely
Wheeler Peak 13,063
Tonopah
Santa Rosa
Davis
Sacramento
Fairfield
Oakland
Stockton
San Francisco
San Jose
Santa Cruz
Monterey
Salinas
Merced
Fresno
Visalia
Mt. Whitney 14,494
Telescope Peak 11,049
Las Vegas
Henderson
San Luis Obispo
Point Arguello
Santa Barbara
Bakersfield
Lancaster
Barstow
Oxnard
LOS ANGELES
Pasadena
Long Beach
Anaheim
San Bernardino
Riverside
Palm Springs
Needles
Oceanside
SAN DIEGO
Tijuana
Mexicali
Ensenada
Punta Colnett
Logan
Ogden
Salt Lake City
Provo
Kings Peak 13,528
Price
Richfield
Moab
Cedar City
St. George
Craig
Fort Collins
Greeley
Sterling
Boulder
Longs Peak 14,255
Denver
Aurora
Grand Junction
Mt. Elbert 14,433
Pikes Pk. 14,110
Colorado Springs
Canon City
Pueblo
Durango
Trinidad
Colby
Hays
Dodge City
Hutchinson
Wichita
Page
Humphreys Peak 12,633
Flagstaff
Prescott
Lake Havasu City
PHOENIX
Mesa
Baldy Peak 11,403
Yuma
Tucson
Sonoyta
Nogales
Agua Prieta
Farmington
Wheeler Peak 13,161
Los Alamos
Gallup
Santa Fe
Mt. Taylor 11,301
Albuquerque
Clovis
Roswell
Silver City
Alamogordo
Las Cruces
Hobbs
Carlsbad
Ciudad Juárez
El Paso
Guadalupe Peak 8,749
Guymon
Amarillo
Oklahoma City
Enid
Stillwater
Norman
Lawton
Plainview
Lubbock
Wichita Falls
Abilene
Fort Worth
Big Spring
Midland
Odessa
Pecos
San Angelo
Fort Stockton
Killeen
Austin
Kerrville
San Antonio
Victoria
Del Rio
Emory Peak 7,825
Nuevo Casas Grandes
Sahuaripa
Ciudad Acuña
Piedras Negras
Nueva Rosita
Nuevo Laredo
Laredo
Kingsville
Monclova
McAllen
Reynosa
Lethbridge
Medicine Hat
Moose Jaw
Regina
Trail
Brandon
ALASKA
CANADA
RUSSIA
YUKON
N.W. TER.
ARCTIC OCEAN
BERING SEA
Gulf of Alaska
BROOKS RANGE
ALASKA RANGE
Utqiagvik
Prudhoe Bay
Beaufort Sea
Nome
Mt. McKinley 20,310
Fairbanks
Anchorage
Valdez
Bethel
Kenai
Kodiak
KODIAK ISLAND
Bristol Bay
Alaska Peninsula
NUNIVAK ISLAND
ST. LAWRENCE ISLAND
Whitehorse
Juneau
Sitka
HAWAII
NI'IHAU
KAUA'I
Līhu'e
Kaua'i Channel
O'AHU
Honolulu
MOLOKA'I
LĀNA'I
MAUI
Kahului
KAHO'OLAWE
HAWAI'I
Mauna Kea 13,796
Hilo
Mauna Loa 13,679
Cape Kumukahi
Kalae

The United States
0 100 200 300 400 Miles
0 100 200 300 400 500 600 Kilometers
Albers Conic Equal Area Projection
M-100115-3
©Rand McNally
CANADA
ONTARIO
QUÉBEC
N.B.
MINNESOTA
WISCONSIN
MICHIGAN
IOWA
ILLINOIS
INDIANA
OHIO
MISSOURI
KENTUCKY
TENNESSEE
ARKANSAS
LOUISIANA
MISSISSIPPI
ALABAMA
GEORGIA
FLORIDA
SOUTH CAROLINA
NORTH CAROLINA
VIRGINIA
WEST VIRGINIA
PENNSYLVANIA
NEW YORK
NEW JERSEY
DELAWARE
MARYLAND
WASHINGTON, DC
CONN.
R.I.
MASS.
VERMONT
NEW HAMP.
MAINE
ATLANTIC OCEAN
Gulf of America
Gulf of Maine
Lake Superior
Lake Michigan
Lake Huron
Lake Erie
Lake Ontario
Georgian Bay
Chesapeake Bay
Delaware Bay
Albemarle Sound
Pamlico Sound
Tampa Bay
Lake Okeechobee
BAHAMAS
Nassau
OZARK PLATEAU
OUACHITA MTS.
ADIRONDACK MTS.
Mt. Mitchell 6,684
Mt. Washington 6,288
Mt. Katahdin 5,268
Cape Cod
Cape Hatteras
Cape Lookout
Cape Fear
Cape Canaveral
Cape Sable
Cape San Blas
NANTUCKET ISLAND
LONG ISLAND
ISLE ROYALE
N
E
S
W
Ottawa
Montréal
Québec
Toronto
Chicago
Detroit
Philadelphia
New York
Boston
Washington, DC
Atlanta
Miami
New Orleans
Nashville
Memphis
Louisville
Indianapolis
Columbus
Cleveland
Pittsburgh
Baltimore
Richmond
Raleigh
Charlotte
Columbia
Jacksonville
Tallahassee
Montgomery
Jackson
Little Rock
Baton Rouge
Birmingham
Milwaukee
Minneapolis
St. Paul
Des Moines
St. Louis
Kansas City
Jefferson City
Springfield
Lansing
Madison
Frankfort
Charleston
Harrisburg
Albany
Hartford
Providence
Concord
Montpelier
Augusta
Trenton
Dover
Annapolis
Tampa
Orlando

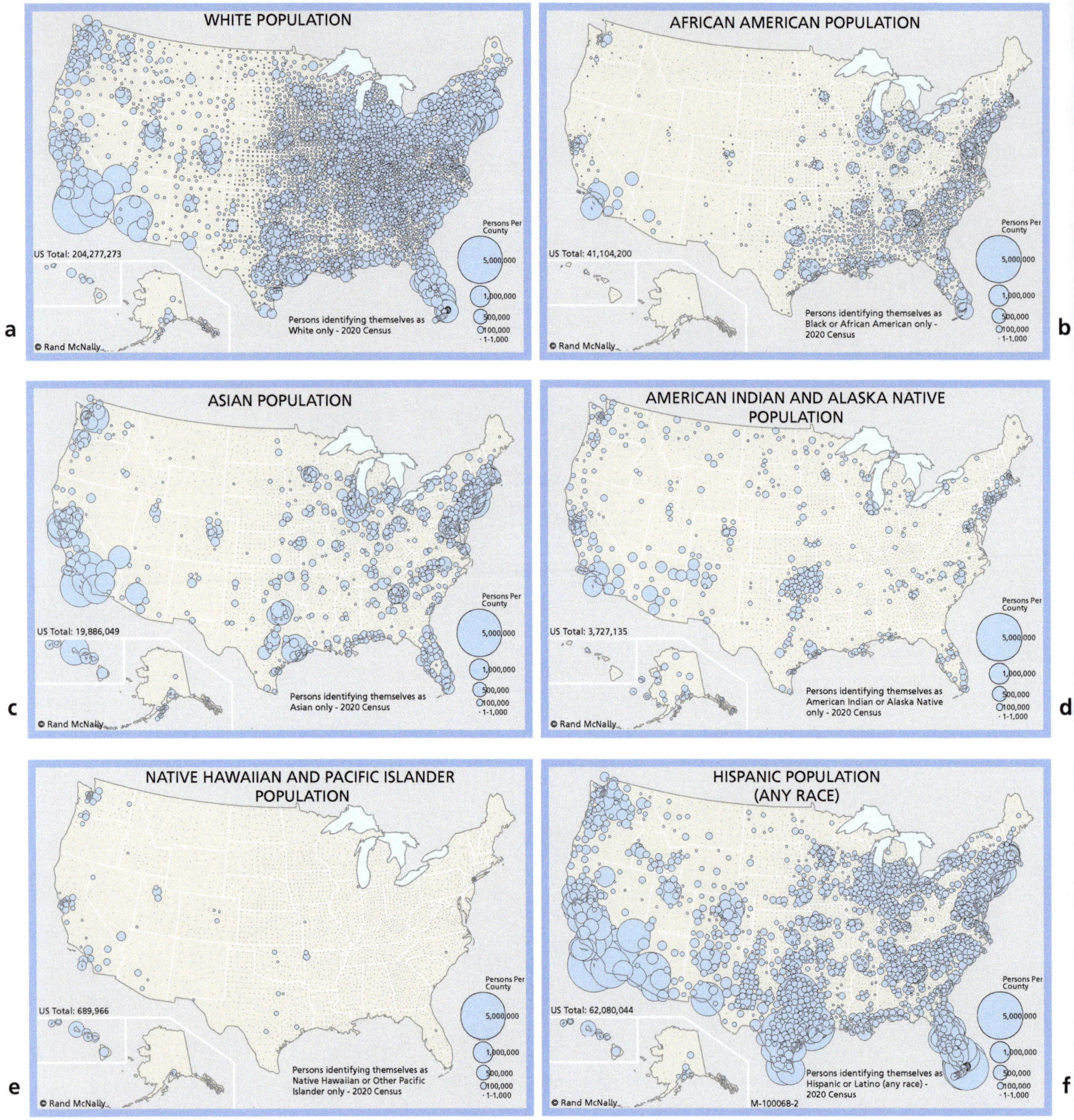

These maps show some major racial and ethnic groups in the United States in 2020 and where they lived.

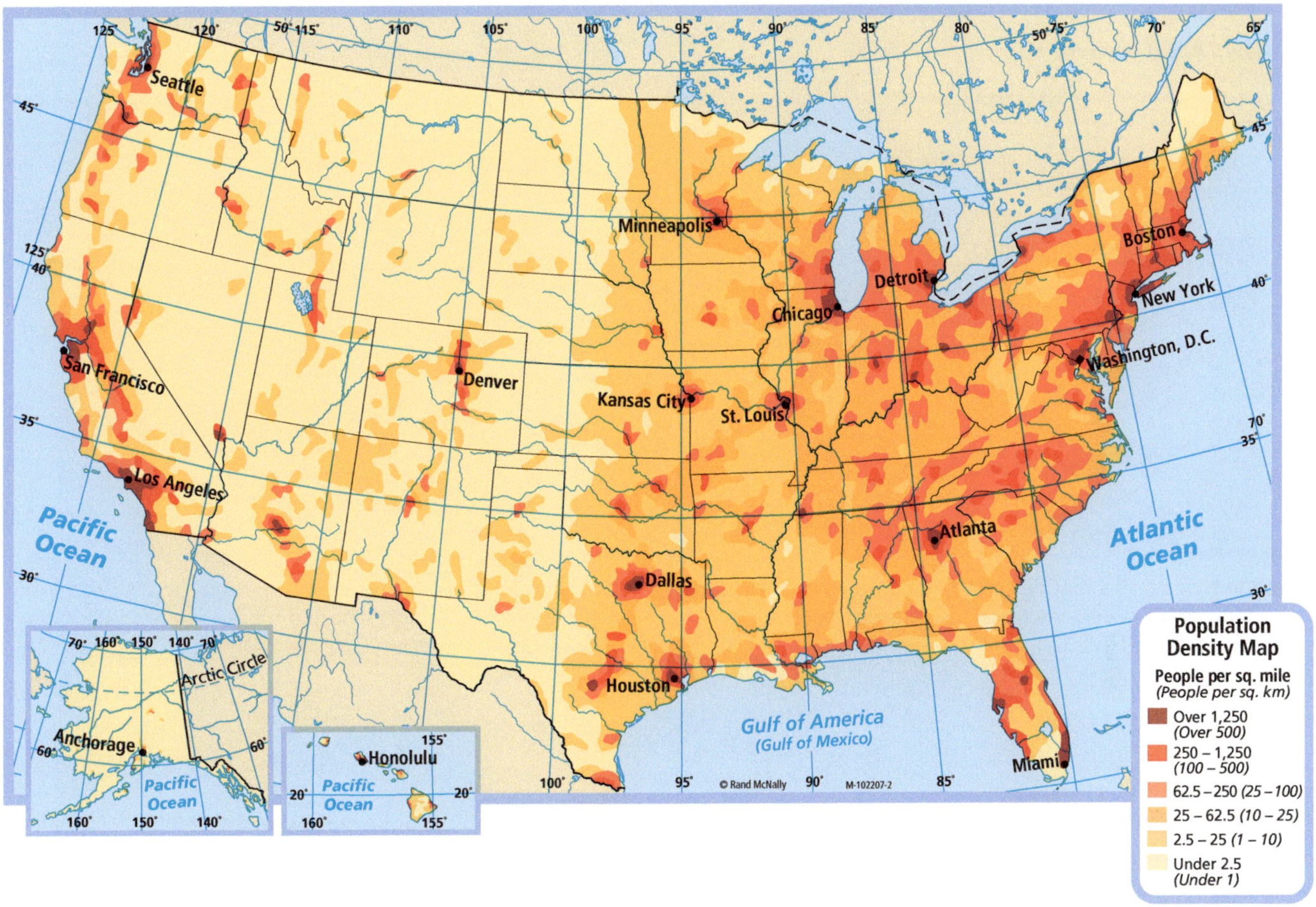

Urban and Rural Population in the United States

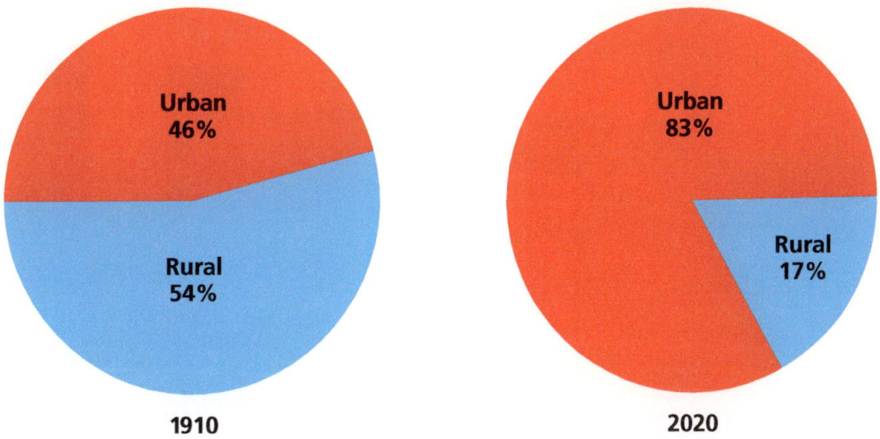

In 2020 more than four-fifths of all Americans lived in urban areas. The map shows the locations of the most densely populated parts of the United States. Notice that several metropolitan areas from Boston to Washington, D.C., have grown together to form a large, densely populated area called a megalopolis. The circle graphs compare the percentages of urban and rural population in the United States in 1910 and 2020.

Median Family Income, 2020

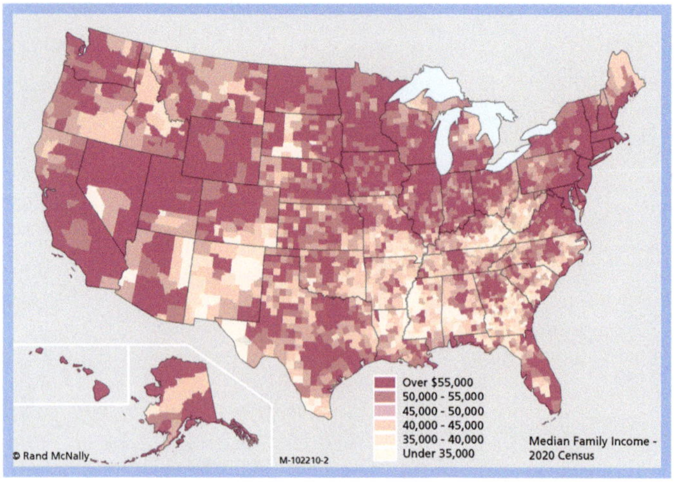

▲ The map shows median family income, or the middle value of all family incomes, in different parts of the United States in 2020.

High School Graduation, 2020

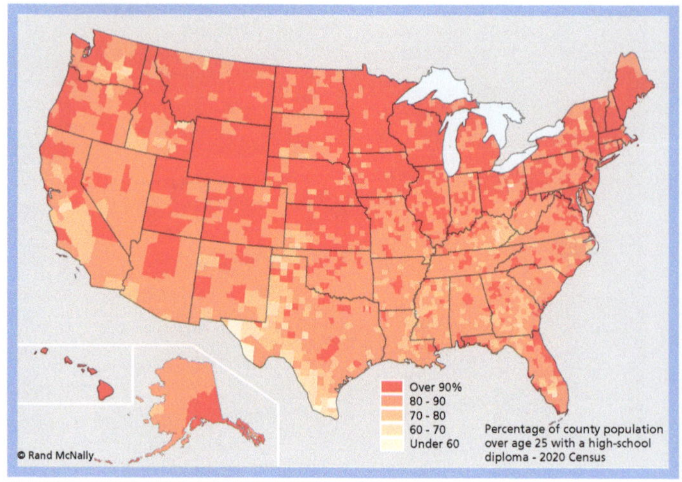

▲ The map shows the percent of people over age 25 who had obtained a high school diploma in different parts of the United States in 2020.

Median Family Income (in current dollars), 1970-2020

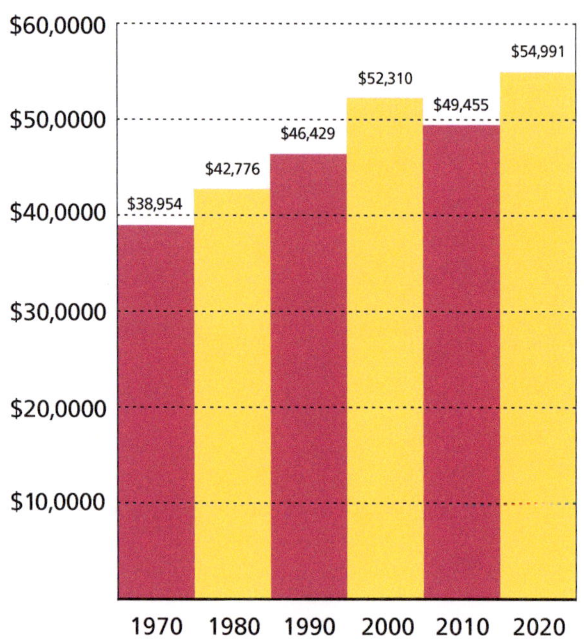

▲ The graph shows how median family income throughout the United States changed between 1970 and 2020.

High School Graduation Statistics, 1970-2020

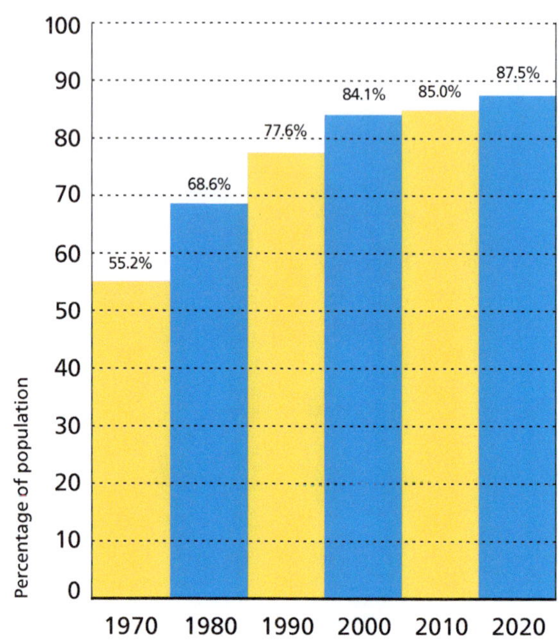

▲ The graph shows how the percentage of persons 25 or older with a high school diploma changed in the United States between 1970 and 2020.

Percentage of U.S. Population Below Poverty Level, 2020

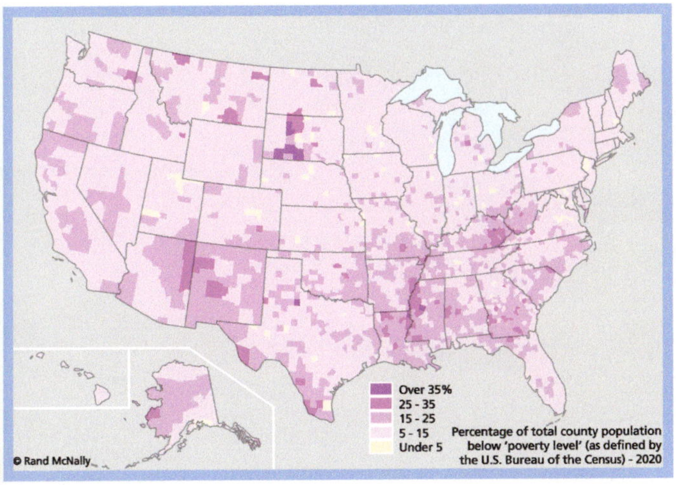

a

▲ The map shows the percentages of people living below the poverty line in different parts of the United States in 2020. Poverty level is based on the income needed to feed a family adequately without spending more than a third of the family income on food.

U.S. Unemployment Rates, 2020

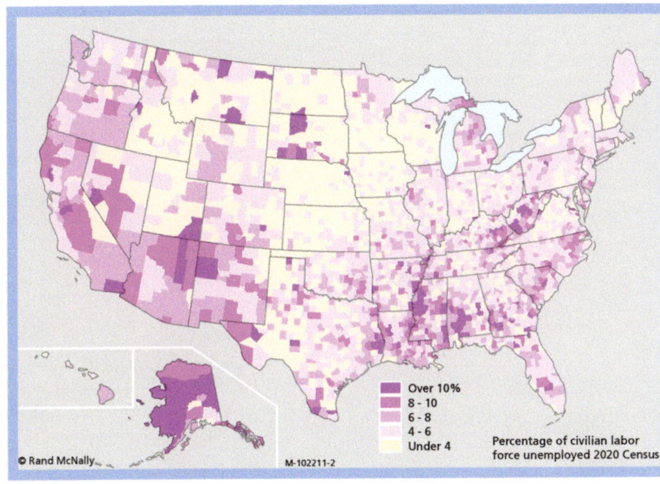

b

▲ The map shows the percentages of unemployed workers in different parts of the United States in 2020.

Percentage of U.S. Population Below Poverty Level, 1970-2020

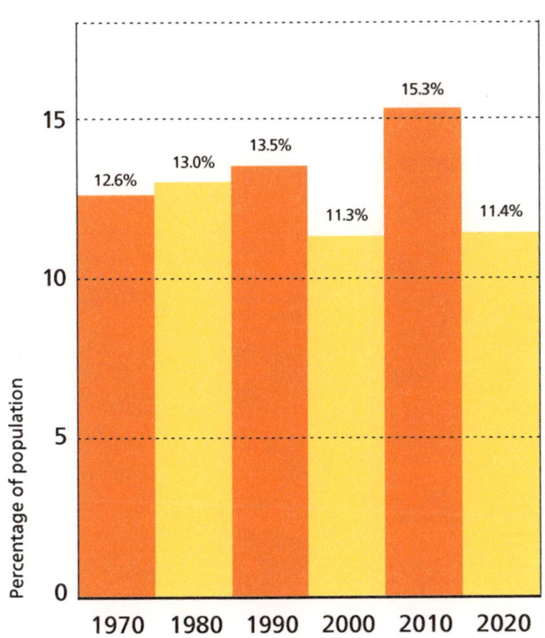

▲ The graph shows how the percentage of Americans below the poverty level changed between 1970 and 2020.

U.S. Unemployment Rates, 1970-2020

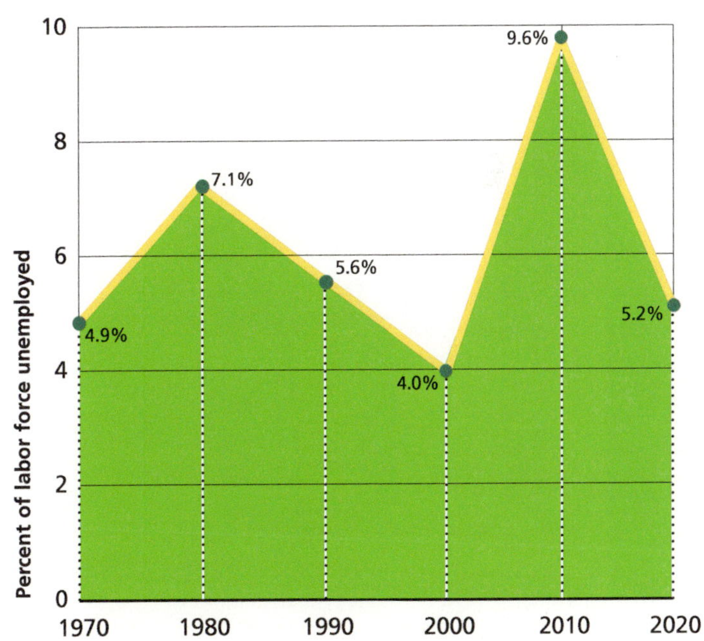

▲ The graph shows how the percentage of unemployed workers in the United States changed between 1970 and 2020.

The World

0 400 800 1200 1600 2000 Miles
0 600 1200 1800 2400 3000 Kilometers
Robinson Projection

M-100116-5 ©Rand McNally

MAP ABBREVIATIONS

Abbr.	Name	Abbr.	Name
ALB.	Albania	HUNG.	Hungary
ARM.	Armenia	KS.	Kosovo
AUS.	Austria	LAT.	Latvia
AZER.	Azerbaijan	LEB.	Lebanon
BEL.	Belguim	LITH.	Lithuania
BHU.	Bhutan	MOLD.	Moldova
BNGL.	Bangladesh	MT.	Montenegro
BUL.	Bulgaria	NETH.	Netherlands
BOS.	Bosnia & Herzegovina	N.M.	North Macedonia
CEN. AFR. REP.	Central Africa Republic	ROM.	Romania
CRO.	Croatia	SERB.	Serbia
CZ.	Czechia	SLO.	Slovenia
DEN.	Denmark	SLVK.	Slovakia
DOM. REP.	Dominican Republic	SWITZ.	Switzerland
GEO.	Georgia	U.A.E.	United Arab Emirates

The 50 states that make up the United States cover an area of more than 3½ million square miles. The United States is the world's third largest country in area.

Arctic polar view

Antarctic polar view

In 2020 the United States had a population of about 330 million. It was the world's third largest country in population, smaller only than India and China.

Populations of United States Colonies and States, 1650-2020

States	1650	1700	1750	1770	1790	1800	1820	1840	1860
Alabama							127,901	590,756	964,201
Alaska									
Arizona									
Arkansas							14,273	97,574	435,450
California									379,994
Colorado									34,277
Connecticut	4,139	25,970	111,280	183,881	237,946	251,002	275,248	309,978	460,147
Delaware	185	2,470	28,704	35,496	59,096	64,273	72,749	78,085	112,216
District of Columbia						8,144	23,336	33,745	75,080
Florida								54,477	140,424
Georgia			5,200	23,375	82,548	162,686	340,989	691,392	1,057,286
Hawaii									
Idaho									
Illinois							55,211	476,183	1,711,951
Indiana						5,641	147,178	685,866	1,350,428
Iowa								43,112	674,913
Kansas									107,206
Kentucky				15,700	73,677	220,955	564,317	779,828	1,155,684
Louisiana							153,407	352,411	708,002
Maine[4]				31,257	96,540	151,719	298,335	501,793	628,279
Maryland	4,504	29,604	141,073	202,599	319,728	341,548	407,350	470,019	687,049
Massachusetts[4]	16,603	55,941	188,000	235,308	378,787	422,845	523,287	737,699	1,231,066
Michigan							8,896	212,267	749,113
Minnesota									172,023
Mississippi						8,850	75,448	375,651	791,305
Missouri							66,586	383,702	1,182,012
Montana									
Nebraska									28,841
Nevada									6,857
New Hampshire	1,305	4,958	27,505	62,396	141,885	183,858	244,161	284,574	326,073
New Jersey		14,010	71,393	117,431	184,139	211,149	277,575	373,306	672,035
New Mexico									93,516
New York	4,116	19,107	76,696	162,920	340,120	589,051	1,372,812	2,428,921	3,880,735
North Carolina		10,720	72,984	197,200	393,751	478,103	638,829	753,419	992,622
North Dakota[3]									
Ohio						45,365	581,434	1,519,467	2,339,511
Oklahoma[5]									
Oregon									52,465
Pennsylvania		17,950	119,666	240,057	434,373	602,365	1,049,458	1,724,033	2,906,215
Rhode Island	785	5,894	33,226	58,196	68,825	69,122	83,059	108,830	174,620
South Carolina		5,704	64,000	124,244	249,073	345,591	502,741	594,398	703,708
South Dakota[3]									4,837
Tennessee				1,000	35,691	105,602	422,823	829,210	1,109,801
Texas									604,215
Utah									40,273
Vermont				10,000	85,425	154,465	235,981	291,948	315,098
Virginia[6]	18,731	58,560	231,033	447,016	691,737	807,557	938,261	1,025,227	1,219,630
Washington									11,594
West Virginia[6]					55,873	78,592	136,808	224,537	376,688
Wisconsin								30,945	775,881
Wyoming									
Total[1]	**50,368**	**250,888**	**1,170,760**	**2,148,076**	**3,929,214**	**5,308,483**	**9,638,453**	**17,069,453[2]**	**31,443,321**

1 All figures prior to 1890 exclude Indians unaffected by the pioneer movement. Figures for 1650 through 1770 include only the British colonies that later became the United States. No areas are included prior to their annexation to the United States. However, many of the figures refer to territories prior to their admission as states. U.S. total includes Alaska from 1880 through 1970 and Hawaii from 1900 through 1970.

2 U.S. total for 1840 includes 6,100 persons on public ships in service of the United States not credited to any state.

3 South Dakota figure for 1860 represents entire Dakota Territory. North and South Dakota figures for 1880 are for the parts of Dakota Territory which later constituted the respective states.

1880	1900	1920	1940	1960	1980	1990	2000	2010	2020
1,262,505	1,828,697	2,348,174	2,832,961	3,266,740	3,893,888	4,062,608	4,447,100	4,779,736	5,024,279
33,426	63,592	55,036	72,524	226,167	401,851	551,947	626,932	710,231	733,391
40,440	122,931	334,162	499,261	1,302,161	2,718,425	3,677,985	5,130,632	6,392,017	7,151,502
802,525	1,311,564	1,752,204	1,949,387	1,786,272	2,286,435	2,362,239	2,673,400	2,915,918	3,011,524
864,694	1,485,053	3,426,861	6,907,387	15,717,204	23,667,565	29,839,250	33,871,648	37,253,956	39,538,223
194,327	539,700	939,629	1,123,296	1,753,947	2,889,735	3,307,912	4,301,261	5,029,196	5,773,714
622,700	908,420	1,380,631	1,709,242	2,535,234	3,107,576	3,295,669	3,405,565	3,574,097	3,605,944
146,608	184,735	223,003	266,505	446,292	594,317	668,696	783,600	897,934	989,948
177,624	278,718	437,571	663,091	763,956	638,432	609,909	572,059	601,723	689,545
269,493	528,542	968,470	1,897,414	4,951,560	9,746,342	13,003,362	15,982,378	18,801,310	21,538,187
1,542,180	2,216,331	2,895,832	3,123,723	3,943,116	5,463,105	6,508,419	8,186,453	9,687,653	10,711,908
	154,001	255,881	422,770	632,772	964,691	1,115,274	1,211,537	1,360,301	1,455,271
32,610	161,772	431,866	524,873	667,191	944,038	1,011,986	1,293,953	1,567,582	1,839,106
3,077,871	4,821,550	6,485,280	7,897,241	10,081,158	11,426,596	11,466,682	12,419,293	12,830,632	12,812,508
1,978,301	2,516,462	2,930,390	3,427,796	4,662,498	5,490,260	5,564,228	6,080,485	6,483,802	6,785,528
1,624,615	2,231,853	2,404,021	2,538,268	2,757,537	2,913,808	2,787,424	2,926,324	3,046,355	3,190,369
996,096	1,470,495	1,769,257	1,801,028	2,178,611	2,364,236	2,485,600	2,688,418	2,853,118	2,937,880
1,648,690	2,147,174	2,416,630	2,845,627	3,038,156	3,660,257	3,698,969	4,041,769	4,339,367	4,505,836
939,946	1,381,625	1,798,509	2,363,880	3,257,022	4,206,312	4,238,216	4,468,976	4,533,372	4,657,757
648,936	694,466	768,014	847,226	969,265	1,125,027	1,233,223	1,274,923	1,328,361	1,362,359
934,943	1,188,044	1,449,661	1,821,244	3,100,689	4,216,975	4,798,622	5,296,486	5,773,552	6,177,224
1,783,085	2,805,346	3,852,356	4,316,721	5,148,578	5,737,037	6,029,051	6,349,097	6,547,629	7,029,917
1,636,937	2,420,982	3,668,412	5,256,106	7,823,194	9,262,078	9,328,784	9,938,444	9,883,640	10,077,331
780,773	1,751,394	2,387,125	2,792,300	3,413,864	4,075,970	4,387,029	4,919,479	5,303,925	5,706,494
1,131,597	1,551,270	1,790,618	2,183,796	2,178,141	2,520,638	2,586,443	2,844,658	2,967,297	2,961,279
2,168,380	3,106,665	3,404,055	3,784,664	4,319,813	4,916,759	5,137,804	5,595,211	5,988,927	6,154,913
39,159	243,329	548,889	559,456	674,767	786,690	803,655	902,195	989,415	1,084,225
452,402	1,066,300	1,296,372	1,315,834	1,411,330	1,569,825	1,584,617	1,711,263	1,826,341	1,961,504
62,266	42,335	77,407	110,247	285,278	800,493	1,206,152	1,998,257	2,700,551	3,104,614
346,991	411,488	443,083	491,524	606,921	920,610	1,113,915	1,235,786	1,316,470	1,377,529
1,131,116	1,883,669	3,155,900	4,160,165	6,066,782	7,364,823	7,748,634	8,414,350	8,791,894	9,288,994
119,565	195,310	360,350	531,818	951,023	1,302,981	1,521,779	1,819,046	2,059,179	2,117,522
5,082,871	7,268,894	10,385,227	13,479,142	16,782,304	17,558,072	18,044,505	18,976,457	19,378,102	20,201,249
1,399,750	1,893,810	2,559,123	3,571,623	4,556,155	5,881,813	6,657,630	8,049,313	9,535,483	10,439,388
36,909	319,146	646,872	641,935	632,446	652,717	641,364	642,200	672,591	779,094
3,198,062	4,157,545	5,759,394	6,907,612	9,706,397	10,797,624	10,887,325	11,353,140	11,536,504	11,799,448
	790,391	2,028,283	2,336,434	2,328,284	3,025,290	3,157,604	3,450,654	3,751,351	3,959,353
174,768	413,536	783,389	1,089,684	1,768,687	2,633,149	2,853,733	3,421,399	3,831,074	4,237,256
4,282,891	6,302,115	8,720,017	9,900,180	11,319,366	11,863,895	11,924,710	12,281,054	12,702,379	13,002,700
276,531	428,556	604,397	713,346	859,488	947,154	1,005,984	1,048,319	1,052,567	1,097,379
995,577	1,340,316	1,683,724	1,899,804	2,382,594	3,121,833	3,505,707	4,012,012	4,625,364	5,118,425
98,268	401,570	636,547	642,961	680,514	690,768	699,999	754,844	814,180	886,667
1,542,359	2,020,616	2,337,885	2,915,841	3,567,089	4,591,120	4,896,641	5,689,283	6,346,105	6,910,840
1,591,749	3,048,710	4,663,228	6,414,824	9,579,677	14,229,288	17,059,805	20,851,820	25,145,561	29,145,505
143,963	276,749	449,396	550,310	890,627	1,461,037	1,727,784	2,233,169	2,763,885	3,271,616
332,286	343,641	352,428	359,231	389,881	551,456	564,964	608,827	625,741	643,077
1,512,565	1,854,184	2,309,187	2,677,773	3,966,949	5,346,818	6,216,568	7,078,515	8,001,024	8,631,393
75,116	518,103	1,356,621	1,736,191	2,853,214	4,132,180	4,887,941	5,894,121	6,724,540	7,705,281
618,457	958,800	1,463,701	1,901,974	1,860,421	1,950,279	1,801,625	1,808,344	1,852,994	1,793,716
1,315,497	2,069,042	2,632,067	3,137,587	3,951,777	4,705,521	4,906,745	5,363,675	5,686,986	5,893,718
20,789	92,531	194,402	250,742	330,066	469,557	455,975	493,782	563,626	576,851
50,189,209	**76,212,168**	**106,021,537**	**132,164,569**	**179,323,175**	**226,547,346**	**249,632,692**	**281,421,906**	**308,745,538**	**334,735,874**

4 Maine figures for 1770 through 1800 are for that area of Massachusetts which became the state of Maine in 1820. Massachusetts figures exclude Maine from 1770 through 1800, but include it from 1650 through 1750. Massachusetts figure for 1650 also includes population of Plymouth (1,566), a separate colony until 1691.

5 Oklahoma figure for 1900 includes population of Indian Territory (392,060).

6 West Virginia figures for 1790 through 1860 are for that area of Virginia which became West Virginia in 1863. These figures are excluded from the figures for Virginia from 1790 through 1860.

Facts About the States

State	Admission to the Union date (order)	Capital	Area in sq.mi. (rank in area)	Nickname	Postal Abbreviation
Alabama	1819 (22)	Montgomery	50,633 (28)	Heart of Dixie	AL
Alaska	1959 (49)	Juneau	570,866 (1)	Last Frontier	AK
Arizona	1912 (48)	Phoenix	113,623 (6)	Grand Canyon State	AZ
Arkansas	1836 (25)	Little Rock	52,024 (27)	Natural State	AR
California	1850 (31)	Sacramento	155,813 (3)	Golden State	CA
Colorado	1876 (38)	Denver	103,610 (8)	Centennial State	CO
Connecticut	1788 (5)	Hartford	4,841 (48)	Constitution State	CT
Delaware	1787 (1)	Dover	1,948 (49)	First State	DE
Florida	1845 (27)	Tallahassee	53,634 (26)	Sunshine State	FL
Georgia	1788 (4)	Atlanta	57,701 (21)	Peach State	GA
Hawaii	1959 (50)	Honolulu	6,421 (47)	Aloha State	HI
Idaho	1890 (43)	Boise	82,623 (11)	Gem State	ID
Illinois	1818 (21)	Springfield	55,499 (24)	Land of Lincoln	IL
Indiana	1816 (19)	Indianapolis	35,817 (38)	Hoosier State	IN
Iowa	1846 (29)	Des Moines	55,839 (23)	Hawkeye State	IA
Kansas	1861 (34)	Topeka	81,737 (13)	Sunflower State	KS
Kentucky	1792 (15)	Frankfort	39,481 (36)	Bluegrass State	KY
Louisiana	1812 (18)	Baton Rouge	43,193 (33)	Pelican State	LA
Maine	1820 (23)	Augusta	30,837 (39)	Pine Tree State	ME
Maryland	1788 (7)	Annapolis	9,709 (42)	Old Line State	MD
Massachusetts	1788 (6)	Boston	7,799 (45)	Bay State	MA
Michigan	1837 (26)	Lansing	56,591 (22)	Wolverine State	MI
Minnesota	1858 (32)	St. Paul	79,605 (14)	North Star State	MN
Mississippi	1817 (20)	Jackson	46,913 (31)	Magnolia State	MS
Missouri	1821 (24)	Jefferson City	68,727 (18)	Show Me State	MO

State	Admission to the Union date (order)	Capital	Area in sq.mi. (rank in area)	Nickname	Postal Abbreviation
Montana	1889 (41)	Helena	145,509 (4)	Treasure State	MT
Nebraska	1867 (37)	Lincoln	76,796 (15)	Cornhusker State	NE
Nevada	1864 (36)	Carson City	109,831 (7)	Silver State	NV
New Hampshire	1788 (9)	Concord	8,951 (44)	Granite State	NH
New Jersey	1787 (3)	Trenton	7,353 (46)	Garden State	NJ
New Mexico	1912 (47)	Santa Fe	121,280 (5)	Land of Enchantment	NM
New York	1788 (11)	Albany	47,111 (30)	Empire State	NY
North Carolina	1789 (12)	Raleigh	48,607 (29)	Tar Heel State	NC
North Dakota	1889 (39)	Bismarck	68,977 (17)	Peace Garden State	ND
Ohio	1803 (17)	Columbus	40,848 (35)	Buckeye State	OH
Oklahoma	1907 (46)	Oklahoma City	68,578 (19)	Sooner State	OK
Oregon	1859 (33)	Salem	95,963 (10)	Beaver State	OR
Pennsylvania	1787 (2)	Harrisburg	44,730 (32)	Keystone State	PA
Rhode Island	1790 (13)	Providence	1,034 (50)	Ocean State	RI
South Carolina	1788 (8)	Columbia	30,056 (40)	Palmetto State	SC
South Dakota	1889 (40)	Pierre	75,790 (16)	Mount Rushmore State	SD
Tennessee	1796 (16)	Nashville	41,227 (34)	Volunteer State	TN
Texas	1845 (28)	Austin	261,194 (2)	Lone Star State	TX
Utah	1896 (45)	Salt Lake City	82,355 (12)	Beehive State	UT
Vermont	1791 (14)	Montpelier	9,215 (43)	Green Mountain State	VT
Virginia	1788 (10)	Richmond	39,472 (37)	Old Dominion	VA
Washington	1889 (42)	Olympia	66,438 (20)	Evergreen State	WA
West Virginia	1863 (35)	Charleston	24,035 (41)	Mountain State	WV
Wisconsin	1848 (30)	Madison	54,153 (25)	Badger State	WI
Wyoming	1890 (44)	Cheyenne	97,063 (9)	Equality State	WY

In addition to place names that appear on the maps in this atlas, the Index also lists names of people, groups, events, and other topics related to American history. It provides explanatory information, such as dates, identifications, and geographic locations for many entries. When appropriate, entries are cross-referenced to related topics.

The Index lists boldfaced page numbers on which each entry appears. A small letter beside a page number identifies a specific map on the page on which the entry appears. Postal abbreviations are used for state names.

The following abbreviations also are used:

Ft.	Fort	St.	Saint
g	graph	t	table
Is.	Islands	terr.	territory
p	photograph	U.S.	United States
pop.	population		

A

B

C

D